TEN ADVENTUROUS WALKS IN BERKSHIRE

Raymond Hugh

Illustrations by
Jackie Hei

ISBN 1 874476 03 9

Published by Morning Mist Publishing 1993
PO Box 108, Reigate, Surrey RH2 9YP
©Raymond Hugh & Jackie Hei 1993

Designed and Printed by
Advanced Data Graphics, Sevenoaks

Every effort is taken in the accuracy of this book. However the author and the publisher cannot accept responsibility for any accidents resulting from the use of this guide.

INDEX

		Pages
	Introduction	i-v
(1)	**Windsor Great Walk** Distance 8 miles (12.75 km)	1 - 9
(2)	**The Water Chase** Distance 8 miles (12.75 km)	10 - 21
(3)	**Romans Revenge** Distance 10¼ miles (16.5 km)	22 - 32
(4)	**The Hungerford Hare** Distance 10¾ miles (17.25 km)	33 - 42
(5)	**Teacher's Test** Distance 11¾ miles (19 km)	43 - 56
(6)	**In Giants' Footsteps** Distance 11¾ miles (19 km)	57 - 68
(7)	**Cox's Choice** Distance 12¾ miles (20.5 km)	69 - 79
(8)	**Escaping the Gallows** Distance 13 miles (21 km)	80 - 89
(9)	**The Lambourn Lunge** Distance 14⅛ miles (22.65 km)	90 - 101
(10)	**The Downland Dare** Distance 16¼ miles (25.25 km)	102 - 111

INTRODUCTION

THE ADVENTURE
The adventure must be yours, it is the thrill of exploration, the pleasure of experiencing something new and the surprise of the unexpected. You could do the same walk several times and each time it will be different. You may surprise a tiny Muntjac deer grazing in a sun soaked clearing. On another occasion, you may see hares racing across the path ahead. On a summer's day the Berkshire Downs are alive with the song of the skylark as it soars above hazy fields of wavering grass. In winter, the song is replaced by the rush of the wind, making your eyes water as it sweeps the downs clear in readiness for spring. The weather can change not only the appearance of a walk, but also the feel. The adventure is discovering the secrets of the route on the day.

THE REWARD
The reward is the sense of achievement and the knowledge that not only have you completed a respectable distance, you will have learned and experienced something of Berkshire which before was a mystery. There is no greater satisfaction than to discover the county as our ancestors did - on foot.

WHEN TO GO
Many walkers make the mistake of only walking in fine weather, leaving the hills at the slightest sign of rain. In wet and windy weather the countryside is untamed and with the majority of the population safe in their houses, one can really get a feeling of remoteness and a better idea of what Berkshire was like several hundred years ago. My suggestion is that you try and do the walks in all seasons and all weathers. At the end if you don't hate me, you will really begin to feel an affinity with the Berkshire countryside and have the satisfaction of knowing the county well. As for the time of day, I recommend that you try and time your walk to include either dawn or dusk. These to me are the best parts of the day, unfortunately, often missed by the majority.

PREPARATION
Planning the walk is as important and enjoyable as doing the walk itself. Firstly, consider whether you want to make a weekend of it. If you do, then I suggest you book local accommodation. This not only cuts down on travelling on the day, but creates a seemingly longer weekend and allows you to remain familiar with the area at night. There is nothing better in my mind than to finish a long walk and retire to local accommodation for a hot bath before a well earned visit to the local village pub, without having to worry about driving home. A selection of recommended accommodation is listed at the end of each walk.

Once you have decided on your walk, familiarise yourself with it. Read the walk through, following it on the map and ensure you understand where it is you are going. The route descriptions contain points of interest and you may want to take time to stop and visit these. If you do, it might be worth borrowing a book from the Library to read up before your visit. Equally, when you have made up your mind on the points of interest to visit, try and estimate the length of your walk. The timings given on each walk are meant as a rough guide only and are based on a person being reasonably fit. If you are unsure, then I suggest you allow for approximately two miles per hour. Timing is important as you could find yourself stumbling back to the start in the dark.

Finally, make sure you are fit. The walks in this book are longer than the average walking book and can be hard work if you are unprepared. To help identify the gradients, a cross section is included at the start of each walk.

WHAT TO TAKE

A good map is essential. I recommend you use the Ordnance Survey Landranger maps and the start of each walk details the map(s) required. You can also use the Ordnance Survey Pathfinder maps which have far more detail such as field boundaries, but they can be harder to find and can ultimately be more expensive.

Once armed with your map, make sure you have sensible clothing. This means clothes which are loose and comfortable. Tight jeans and high heels are not recommended! No matter how good the weather is at the start of the day, always pack some waterproofs. Being caught out in the rain without the necessary protection is not an experience I would recommend. In summer if you are walking in shorts, waterproof trousers are also particularly useful as a temporary protection against nettles. There is a wide range of waterproof clothing now available. The two recommendations I would make are:-

(1) Make sure you are completely covered, that is buy trousers and a jacket.

(2) Buy clothing made from one of the breathable materials - your local stockist will advise you on these.

If the weather is cold, then gloves and a hat are always advisable. No matter what time of year, I always pack a jumper and have never regretted it. Keeping warm helps avoid tiredness. Most importantly, make sure you have a good pair of shoes. If you can afford it, then buy a pair of walking boots. If not, then make sure your shoes are strong, comfortable and have soles with a good grip.

Equally important are good socks. If you have boots then two pairs are advisable. Do not think that the socks you wear to the office will do!

Sensibly clothed, you can now think about other equipment you may need. A camera and a pair of binoculars are always useful and can enhance your day out. I always carry a pocket book on birds, you could do the same or add to this with a book on local flora or history. You will find the walk all the more enjoyable for a little bit of knowledge. Do not though, get over enthusiastic and take a library or you may find yourself requiring a book on first aid!

A basic first aid kit however, is always advisable. The Berkshire countryside may appear tame and so it is compared to the Himalayas, but it must still be treated with respect. The book and the map should be enough to find the route without difficulty, however a compass is always useful for finding your way when paths are undefined.

Refreshments are always an important consideration. There are places where you can get a bite to eat on every walk, but even if you wish to use these facilities, it is important to carry some basic snacks, especially in cold weather. You should always carry water and a thermos flask with a hot drink or soup can also be very welcome.

To carry everything you need for your walk, I recommend you invest in a comfortable day sack or small rucksack. These are now available from a wide assortment of shops, but before you make your purchase, make sure it is strong and more importantly, that it is comfortable.

Finally, take your five senses with you - these are essential if you are to fully appreciate the walk but, most importantly, **ENSURE YOU TAKE THIS BOOK!**

GETTING THERE

Most people will be mobile, i.e. a car or bicycle. Where practical, I have listed railway stations. Buses however, are far more difficult as their routes and timetables tend to change with the wind. For those people relying on a bus to reach the start, I have listed the main bus companies serving the area.

Martins (Tel: 0494 711298)

Bee Line (Tel: 0628 21344)

Newbury Buses (Tel: 0635 40743)

Oxford to Victoria (Tel: 0865 727000)

National Express (Tel: 0865 781579)

Reading Buses (Tel: 0734 509509)

For information of rail services, telephone Network South East on - 0734 595911.

ROUTE FINDING

The route descriptions are instructional rather than poetic and should be followed without difficulty. To assist you, a series of symbols in the left hand margin enable you to identify specific points on the walk at a glance. A good map is essential and should be used in conjunction with the route description. Please remember that like everything else, the countryside changes with time, e.g. a fenced path can become unfenced and vice versa.

Before setting out, make sure you have identified the route on the map. To pinpoint a starting point or place of interest and key points on the route, I have used grid references which are printed in bold in the text. These are six figured numbers which identify a particular point on the map. Every Ordnance Survey map is covered by a national grid. The grid's lines are identified by numbers printed on the map's surround. To find a grid reference, take the first three numbers, which refer to the vertical lines on your map and locate them on the top or bottom (north or south) of the map. The third number is an imaginary line in the square following the first two numbers. To find this line, divide the square into ten equal parts. Then take the last three numbers, which refer to the horizontal lines and locate them on the left or right (east or west) of your map and follow the line of this reference until it meets the line of the first reference. Their meeting point is the grid reference point itself. Do not rely on the maps in this book, these are not to scale and are meant as a rough guide only.

It is important that you recognise the various types of footpath signs. Most are fairly obvious, i.e. wooden post with a sign marked "footpath" or "public bridleway", pointing in the direction of the right of way. Some will have the name of a specific route, for example, "The Ridgeway".

Over recent years many County Councils have standardised their signs to follow national guidelines. Footpaths are now shown with a yellow arrow and bridleways with a blue one. Like the old wooden signs, the arrows will point in the direction of the right of way. Some arrows will have the initials of a recognised walk imprinted, though this is still rare in Berkshire. On top of all this, you will often find custom built signs. These can mark an official route, but more often than not, are the work of local farmers guiding the walker across their land. An example of the former is the Lambourn Valley Way, which has the name of the route encircling the relevant directional arrow.

An important rule on route finding is to take your time. Follow the map and read the route description thoroughly. If you do this, then you will return to base without mishap.

LONG DISTANCE WALKS

Many of the routes in this book meet long distance linear walks which run through Berkshire. In case you want to try any, I have listed their names and distances below, together with the publisher who produces a description of the walk.

Bristol to London Walk - 172 miles (Ramblers Association)

Grand Union Canal Walk - 145 miles (British Waterways)

Inkpen Way - 62 miles (Thornhill Press)

King Alfred's Way - 108 miles (Thornhill Press)

Lambourn Valley Way - 22 miles (Berkshire County Council - leaflet)

London Countryway - 205 miles (Constable)

Maidenhead Boundary Walk - 18 miles (East Berks Ramblers Association)

Ramblers Route - 26 miles (Bracknell Forest Borough Council)

The Ridgeway Path - 85 miles (H.M.S.O.)

The Three Castles Path - 60 miles (East Berks Ramblers Association)

Test Way - 44 miles (Hampshire County Council)

Thames Walk - 156 miles (Ramblers Association)

Wayfarers Walk - 70 miles (Hampshire County Council)

TOURIST INFORMATION CENTRES

If you require any further information on transport, tourist facilities or accommodation, I have listed the local Tourist Information Centres below.

Maidenhead (Tel: 0628 781110)

Newbury (Tel: 0635 30267)

Reading (Tel: 0734 566226)

Windsor (Tel: 0753 852010)

AUTHOR'S NOTE

Every effort has been made to ensure that the route descriptions are accurate. Time changes things however and can alter the description of the route. If you have any difficulty in finding any part of a route, please write with details giving a grid reference, to enable me to re-examine the directions. A free copy of the next publication will be forwarded for any suggestions used in the next edition.
Enjoy your walks.

WINDSOR GREAT WALK

Distance: 8 miles (12.75 km)
Time: Allow approximately 4½ hours
Map: Ordnance Survey Landranger Map 175 (also recommended for this walk is Footpath Map 8 by the East Berkshire Ramblers Association)

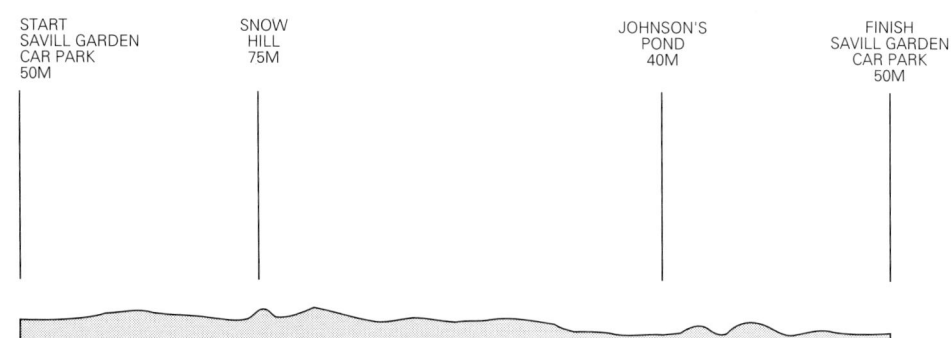

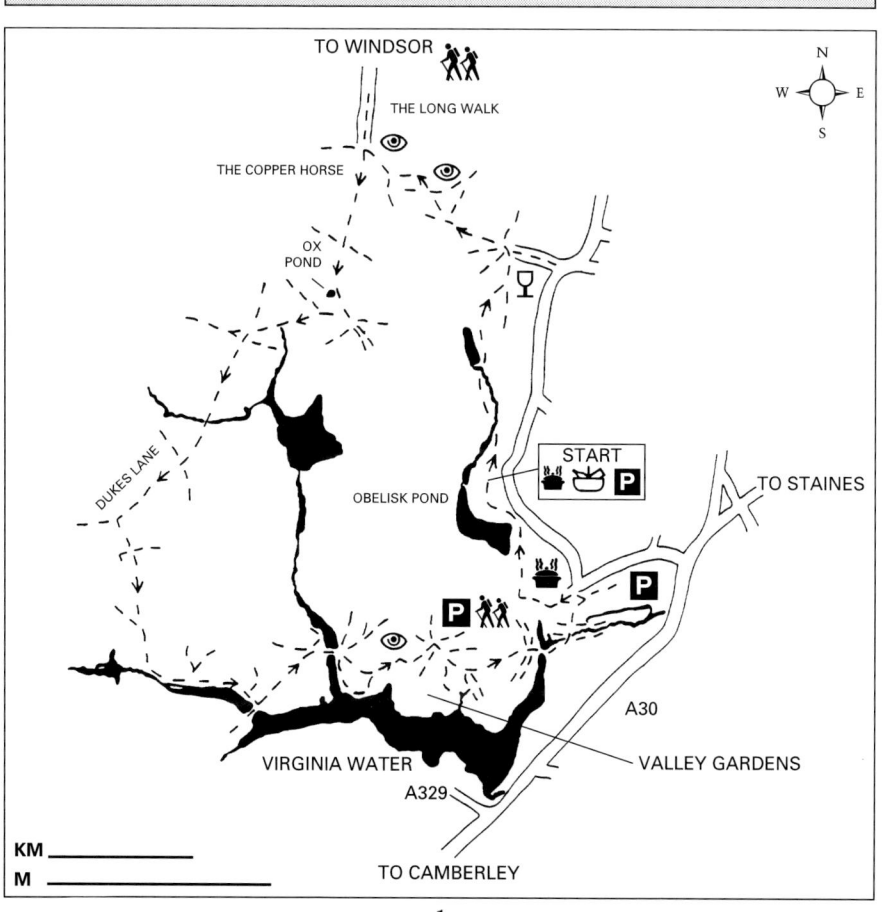

START	SNOW	JOHNSON'S	FINISH
SAVILL GARDEN	HILL	POND	SAVILL GARDEN
CAR PARK	75M	40M	CAR PARK
50M			50M

Walk Summary

Although a walk around a park can hardly be described as adventurous, the unique landscape and history of Windsor Great Park cannot be ignored by any walking book on Berkshire. The walk is also a good introduction for people who enjoy walking but are a little nervous of tackling a walk which is more than just a few miles long. The route itself escorts the walker around most of the highlights of the park with, in places, some surprisingly good views. The final stretch takes you through the world famous Valley Gardens and along the banks of Virginia Water. The best time of year to do the walk is in late spring or early summer when the park is at its most spectacular. The majority of the walk is along well established paths. However, just because they are in a park does not mean you will escape the mud. Many of the paths are used as rides for horses and therefore can get churned up. Turning up in a pair of trainers after a period of wet weather is definitely a mistake - bring those boots!

Start - OS. 977706 Map 175

The walk starts from the Savill Garden car park marked by a blue "P" on the Ordnance Survey Landranger map. The car park is open from dawn to dusk so make sure you allow plenty of time to avoid an unexpected extra walk into town. There is a charge which is at least £ 1 (at the time of writing). However, spending a small amount at the souvenir shop, which is not difficult, entitles you to free parking.

To get there, if coming from the south, take the M3 to exit at junction 3 and follow the signs for Bracknell on the A322. After one mile, take the A30, signposted to London, Staines and Heathrow. Stay on the A30 to go through Sunningdale passing over a level crossing and later pass a well known landmark, "The Wheatsheaf" pub. After "The Wheatsheaf", you will see signs for Savill Garden, take the next turning left, Wick Road, and follow this passing the entrance to the Valley Gardens car park, until you reach the well signposted car park for Savill Garden.

If coming from the north, make your way to Windsor and from there take the A308, signposted to Staines and the Savill Garden. At a large roundabout, continue to follow signs for the A308, Staines and Savill Garden. Go through Old Windsor and at a second roundabout turn right, signposted to Englefield as well as the Savill Garden. Follow this road until you see a sign pointing right for the Savill Garden and The Great Park. Take this, Castle Hill Road, and at a crossroads turn right again. Follow the lane to later turn left into Wick Lane which is signposted to Savill Garden, and follow Wick Lane to reach the Savill Garden car park.

An alternative start can be made from the Valley Gardens car park or from Windsor itself by taking The Long Walk, though the latter will add six miles to your walk. The nearest railway station is at Windsor which connects with the main line at Slough.

WINDSOR GREAT WALK

Before starting the walk, it is worth knowing a little bit about the park itself.

Windsor Great Park. *The name is very apt for "great" this park certainly is. Great in beauty, grandeur, history, wildlife and charm. Over the years, it has been sculptured by our monarchs as a fitting garden for the castle at Windsor and yet perhaps the park's greatest asset is its natural beauty. For this we have to thank William the Conqueror who first created the park by awarding the forest, which then covered southern Berkshire, northern Hampshire and Surrey, royal status. As a royal forest, it was protected under forest law to preserve its wildlife and in particular, game for the royals to hunt. The forest law is the first known attempt at conservation* in this country. It was rigorously upheld and offenders were severely punished, the ultimate punishment being death for killing a stag. Whatever your view of this, the law was effective and responsible for not only the unique landscape here at Windsor, but the New Forest and the Forest of Dean.

Over the years, the forest served many purposes other than hunting. In the reign of Queen Elizabeth I, oaks were planted as they were in the New Forest, to provide timber for shipbuilding. Some of these trees escaped going to sea and are still present today. Oliver Cromwell used the forest as a training ground for his New Model Army, responsible for finally defeating the Royalists. I have always thought it the ulimate insult that these anti-royal troops perfected their methods in the most royal of parks.

The reinstatement of the monarchy in the form of King Charles II, also saw the start of the conversion of the forest into the park we know today. The first step came in 1680, when work started on The Long Walk, a three mile drive which spectacularly connects Windsor Castle with the park. Since then, every monarch has added to the park, though it is King George III who must be credited for most of the park's current layout and many of its monuments.

Today, the park provides a valuable haven for wildlife. Its many oaks support a wealth of insect life and deer still roam under their boughs. For the botanist, there are the world famous Valley and Savill Gardens, a pleasure at any time of year.

There are several exits from the car park. To start our walk, you must take the second exit from the left, that is the second exit from the car park entrance. If by chance you do take one of the other exits, then simply follow the signs to the Savill Garden Restaurant and Shop to rejoin our route.

From the car park follow the signs to the Shop in Savill Garden (not the totem pole), to almost immediately come out in front of the Obelisk, a huge monument overlooking a tranquil pond, the Obelisk Pond.

The Obelisk (OS. 976705 Map 175) *was errected, as a plaque confirms, at the command of King George II to commemorate the military success of his son, William, Duke of Cumberland, later George III. What the plaque does not tell you is that the military success was the controversial Battle of Culloden (1746), in which Bonnie Prince Charles' Highlanders were literally massacred by the English. The battle followed a daring invasion of England by the Prince, encouraged by promised support from France. The Prince's army got as far as Derby before the English organised themselves and sent two huge armies to meet him. On 6th December, 1745, the Scots started an organised retreat, returning behind their own border. Even now, the Prince had not given up hope and set about raising new recruits. Eventually, the two armies met at Culloden. The Scots were, in the main, young, hopelessly outnumbered and lacked the weapons at the disposal of the English army. In a huge gamble, the Highlanders simply charged the English, tactics being thrown to the wind. Experienced and well trained, the English army were merciless in their slaughter and over one thousand Highlanders died. The young Scottish Prince escaped to Skye and on to France, where Europe turned its back on him.*

The battle caused uproar in England as well as Scotland and earned the Duke the nickname, "Butcher Cumberland". Today, the site of the Battle of Culloden is preserved by the Scottish National Trust. Apart from the Obelisk, as a reward, the then Duke was made Ranger of Windsor Great Park and it is him we must thank for much of its layout today.

There are several benches on the lawn surrounding the Obelisk, which make a pleasant if early place to pause and admire the pond.

Do not walk to the pond, but turn right onto a tarmac path just beyond the Obelisk and follow this in the direction of the signs to Savill Garden and Shop. Pass the Savill Garden Restaurant and Shop on your left, the latter selling a number of souvenirs and plants grown in the gardens.

The Savill Garden (OS. 976708 Map 175) *until 1932 did not exist. In that year one Eric Savill joined the staff at the park as Deputy Surveyor. The garden then was part of a nursery which supplied the park with many of its younger trees and was known as The Bog Garden - no explanation required! Eric Savill started on the reconstruction of the garden almost immediately. He was encouraged, he said, by a remark made by King George V and Queen Mary, that "the garden is very small Mr. Savill, but very nice". After this, he was determined to perfect a greater garden. The result is for all to see and is now world famous. For his efforts, he was promoted to Deputy Ranger and became Sir Eric Savill in 1951. But perhaps the tribute he cherished most was that given by King George VI, who commanded the name of the garden to be changed from The Bog Garden to the Savill Garden, reward indeed considering the remarks made by the King's father. I will not attempt to describe the garden, except to say that the reward given to Sir Eric was more than just and a visit to the park would not be complete without some time spent enjoying the results of his labours.*

From the shop and restaurant continue along the tarmac drive, now running between rhodedendron and laurel bushes. As the drive bends left beside a nursery, you should leave it to continue straight on along a farm track which runs in a straight line between the now familiar rhodedendron bushes. This is the famous rhodedendron ride created by George IV and in May and June the blooms provide a magnificent spectacle.

Sometime on and after passing over a small brick bridge, you will meet a crossing track which you should ignore to continue straight on. After a short distance, the rhodedendrons give way on the the left affording views over a small pond frequented by ducks. Perhaps the most attractive of these is the richly coloured mandarin duck, introduced from Asia in the late 1920's. The mandarin duck is now recognised as a bird living naturally in the British Isles and is particularly prevalent here at Windsor Great Park. Should you wish to take a rest here, there are seats carved from tree trunks around the pond.

Stay on the track later ignoring a track off to the right to continue ahead. The rhodedendrons eventually give way and you will shortly pass a huge redwood tree. After this, the track leads to a wooden gate through which you should pass and thereafter, bear right to follow the perimeter of a gatehouse, "Bishopsgate Lodge". Turning right at this point, would take you out of the park to arrive at "The Fox and Hounds", a very attractive Courage pub offering good beer and a selection of food.

Our route however, is left at "Bishopsgate Lodge" to join a tarmac drive heading for some pink buildings in the distance which are the gates to the Royal Lodge. Thirty paces on after joining the tarmac drive, bear right off the drive and follow a path running through oak trees. This follows perimeter fencing to the deer park on the right and, as you join the path, you should ignore a set of metal gates into the deer park on the same side.

Continue ahead along the path with the grand entrance to the Royal Lodge ahead to your left, to reach another set of metal gates directly ahead which lead into the deer park (these are almost level with the Royal Lodge entrance on your left). Pass through the gates and follow a tarmac drive ahead along the left hand side of a valley which sweeps round to the right. Soon after, you will pass a small group of trees on the left with cross country horse jumps. At the base of the trees is a small plaque stating "Queen Victoria 1866".

The Deer at Windsor Great Park. *As you continue, be forever watchful for a glimpse of a herd of Red deer which live in the park. The Red deer have only recently returned after being removed from the park during the Second World War, justice indeed if you consider that the park probably would not even be here if it wasn't for the deer. Outside the deer park, especially near Virginia Water, you may catch sight of other variety of deer. In particular, the tiny Roe deer, a small herd of which was released into Windsor forest in 1850 by Prince Albert. These were a gift and came from the famous deer park at Petworth in West Sussex. Incidentally, if you spot a deer which appears to glow, you could be witnessing Herne's ghost. The ghost is said to appear in human form with the skin of a deer and a helmet made from the skull of a stag complete with antlers. Herne was a famous hunter and forester to Richard II. It is far more probable however that the story is connected with an ancient pagan hunters dance called the Horn Dance, in which hunters paraded in just such attire.*

The drive later begins to bear left and reaches the crest of a hill, where the valley you have been following opens out to afford superb views across the Thames valley, Windsor Castle and the deer park. Stay on the drive, now descending, to pass over a very grand stone bridge of some size, particularly when one sees the size of the stream it crosses. After this, you will gain your first views of a statue known as The Copper Horse on your left and the tree lined Long Walk from Windsor Castle on your right.

The tarmac drive you have been following soon meets the Long Walk. It is possible to turn right here and follow the Long Walk to visit Windsor. In fact, I can think of no better way to approach Windsor, albeit this will invite a detour of approximately six miles and is perhaps better left as just a romantic idea. To continue on our route, leave the drive turning left along a grass track heading up Snow Hill to the foot of The Copper Horse, which stands on a false mound of rocks. On reaching the statue you will enjoy probably the best views over Windsor Great Park and to the north, Windsor Castle and the deer park.

Apart from an inscription in latin, there is nothing here to inform you of the statue's purpose, so perhaps I can oblige.

The Copper Horse (OS. 967727 Map 175) *was erected by George IV in 1831 in memory of his father George III. The statue which is by Westmacott, depicts the King clothed in a Roman toga astride a horse. On its mound, the statue stands fiftysix feet high and on top of Snow Hill, the highest point in the park, can be seen from miles around. Errecting it was not easy. At one point, one of the horse's legs broke off and to repair it a furnace had to be set up at the top of the hill. Whilst this was* happening, the twelve men employed in errecting the statue had to shelter inside it from inclement weather. As previously mentioned, from the statue one has a perfect view of the Long Walk and Windsor Castle. The trees bordering the Long Walk, were once elms which have since been replaced by horse chestnuts and London planes. Of these, there are one thousand, six hundred and fifty, all exactly thirty feet apart.

Recently, Snow Hill has acted as a show piece for celebration. In 1977, the Queen lit a bonfire here to celebrate her silver jubilee and another was lit in 1981 to celebrate the wedding of Charles and Diana.

i Walk round the statue and continue straight on along the grass track the other side, heading south and directly away from Windsor Castle. The grass track leads down the southern slope of Snow Hill, where ahead to your left a magnificent pink building will come into view, the Royal Lodge. The Royal Lodge was much favoured by George IV, who used it as a summer residence as well as his home during his final years. Descend to pass through a metal gate and continue in the same direction along a now hedged track. This part of the walk can be very wet and muddy in winter.

After a short distance, you will meet a wide crossing track. The turning left here is private and leads to the Royal Lodge. To continue our route however, go over the crossing track and carry straight on, where soon after you will pass two clumps of trees, perfectly round, on your right. Follow the track gently uphill through a small strip of woodland and pass a pond known as the Ox Pond (a hint as to its original purpose), on the right. Ignore any turnings off and stay on the track to eventually reach a tarmac drive in front of "Chaplains Lodge" (ahead to your right). Also ahead of you here is the royal school.

Turn right along the tarmac drive passing "Chaplains Lodge" and note a sign on the left informing you that you are now heading for the village shop. The drive quickly descends and bends right where you should leave it to take a smaller drive left at a fork. Follow this downhill where as a guide, to your left is one of the farms in the park and continue to cross over a small stream to go uphill once more.

On meeting a crossing drive which is in fact a lane **(OS. 959716)**, turn left to shortly meet a crossroads which this time you should ignore to continue ahead, now following Dukes Lane. Immediately after, pass to the right of some houses and stay on the lane going gently downhill, running between fields and a border of oaks.

i **The Oak Trees at Windsor.** *The oak has always, along with the deer, been the life blood of the park and some of the oaks are reputed to be over five hundred years old. An iron marker on Dukes Lane, states that the oaks here were planted in 1751. Apart from wood for shipbuilding and house timbers, they also provided firewood, fodder and fencing for the local people who used the park to graze their animals. A common practice was "pollarding", which takes the form of cutting an oak's lower boughs out of reach of grazing animals. It was then from the new growth that fencing and fodder was collected. Trees on which this was practised became known as Pollard oaks and are easily recognisable from the oaks which have been left to grow of their own accord. For the naturalist, the oak is probably the most important tree in the British Isles. An adult tree, apart from providing nesting sites for birds and food for small mammals, acts as a home to literally thousands of small insects.*

You should now follow Dukes Lane for approximately one mile, ignoring a drive off to the left, shortly after which you should cross a small stream. Thereafter, and just prior to a gatehouse on the ridge ahead, turn left onto a track which leads through woodland, a pleasant change after the open fields of the past few miles. The woodland, well established beech and oaks, is full of birds and if you are fortunate enough to see it, other wildlife.

After a short distance you will pass railings on the left and then a track off to the left which you should ignore. After this, pass over a stream and ignore another track off to the right to continue your route ahead along the main track through the wood. Eventually, the track meets a turning left which goes immediately over a stream and is signposted as "no entry for horses or cycles". Take this over the stream and follow the track as it bends right thereafter. The trees at this point above your head, are full of mistletoe, a rare sight these days.

Mistletoe - once used by Druids to increase a woman's fertility

Mistletoe. *In pagan times, mistletoe was much revered and was said to have the power to increase fertility in a woman, something that was vital as child mortality then would have been very high and having large families ensured the survival of a community. Very often, it was the powerful Druids who mixed the fertility potions using mistletoe. They also used it in many of their sacred rites. Pliny the Elder, writing almost two thousand years ago, describes how the Druids cut down the mistletoe with golden sickles. The mistletoe had to be caught in a Druid's white robe, as it was believed that any contact with the ground would immediately drain the powers from the plant. It is from this ancient fertility practice that the modern tradition of kissing under the mistletoe originates. Up until the last century, a man could only have as many kisses as there were berries on the twig. Thankfully, this restriction has since died out and nowadays, the mistletoe can be used to ask for a kiss, berries or not!*

i

The track, now wide and grass, follows the left hand ridge of a valley where on your right you can see the stream crossed earlier now opening out into a lake, the beginnings of Virginia Water.

Virginia Water *is another feature, created by George III, in the park. When made Ranger in 1746, he appointed the Sandby brothers to help landscape the park. To thank his army for victory at the Battle of Culloden, he offered much of the manual labour involved in the landscaping to many of his old soldiers. One of the Sandby brother's first and most notable creations was the making of a large lake from a bog, Virginia Water. The lake is cleverly designed to appear larger than it is. It is in fact, two miles long and covers just over one hundred and sixty acres. The lake also acts as a drainage system for the surrounding gardens. To naturalise the lake, George III ordered extensive woodland to be planted, most of it naturalised broadleaf, with a few exotics as well as some firs and pine. Today, this clever planting can be seen to its full effect, the woodland appearing as old as the great forest itself. Later George IV had a minature frigate built for the lake on which he would frequently ride. This unfortunately disappeared during the reign of Queen Victoria.*

i

You will eventually meet a drive on your right which crosses the lake by way of a magnificent stone bridge, the High Bridge. Our route however, is left along another drive going away from the lake, to soon after ignore another drive off to the right which leads to some houses visible across a green. After a short distance, the drive bends right to cross an arm of the lake. Ignore a track off to the right at this point and stay on the drive to soon after take the second track right, signposted as Lakeside Walk.

After approximately twenty paces, turn left and go gently uphill along a path signposted to the Valley Gardens. You will immediately enter a variety of rhodedendron bushes which in spring and early summer are a mass of colour. Welcome to the Valley Gardens.

i **The Valley Gardens (OS. 975695 Map 175),** *as with the Savill Garden, were the creation of Sir Eric Savill. The gardens were started in 1947, the first job being to clear the thick undergrowth and the dense woodland, much of it planted by George III. The pride and joy of the gardens is a unique collection of rhodedendron bushes recognised by many as the greatest collection in the world. The base of the collection came from a garden in Ascot created by one J. B. Stevenson. The gardens are also known for their magnolias, some of which are the largest I have ever seen. The best time to see the gardens is May or June, so if you are walking this way outside of these months, promise yourself a return visit.*

Approximately thirty paces on, the path forks and you should take the right hand path where, after another twenty metres, you should join a track coming in from the left to continue ahead. The rhodedendrons soon give way on your right here to afford excellent views over Virginia Water. On your left is a grass path which leads up through a mixture of heathers and firs.

Continue along the track ignoring any further turnings off and pass the national rhodedendron species collection on the left and the national holly collection on your right. Both are signposted. The track eventually leads down into a valley where it becomes more prominent and graduates into gravel, to lead up the other side winding as it goes. Nearing the top you will pass a number of benches set back from the track and also at this point, see a mass of minor paths which if you have time, are a delight to explore through the gardens.

At a junction of tracks beside the heather garden on your left, take the second track right signposted to the totem pole to again pass a stunning display of rhodedendrons on your right. On your left, is a perfect lawn which gives way to firs and a bench where you can take a rest. After some distance, the track forks beneath a giant redwood tree. Here you should take the left hand track to lead across more open ground, parted by firs, and descend heading for the totem pole, now in view in the distance.

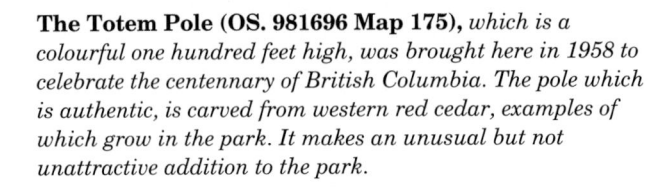

i **The Totem Pole (OS. 981696 Map 175),** *which is a colourful one hundred feet high, was brought here in 1958 to celebrate the centenary of British Columbia. The pole which is authentic, is carved from western red cedar, examples of which grow in the park. It makes an unusual but not unattractive addition to the park.*

At the totem pole you will meet a junction of tracks, where you should continue straight on in the direction of Wick Road car park which is signposted. Once again, you will soon cross Virginia Water, a lovely spot especially in summer. Leave the track immediately after and turn left to follow the right hand bank of what is now Wick Pond, heading for a white bridge in the distance. Cross the bridge and take the path which forks right, uphill through some woods and ignore any minor paths off to the left or right including a crossing path.

On reaching the top of the hill, turn right and go away from the lake along a wide grass track. This leads you to a tarmac drive onto which you should turn left to almost immediately after, pass the "Bailiwick Restaurant" at Cheesemans Gate. Ignore the exit from the park at this point and continue ahead, now going gently downhill. As you progress, the drive bends right to cross a stream and shortly after, you should ignore a track off to the right to continue your route in the direction of the signs to the Valley Gardens.

The drive now takes you steadily uphill where you should look out for a crossing track which is not tarmac (if you find yourself meeting a tarmac crossing drive, then you will have gone too far and should retrace your steps). Turn right onto the crossing track and follow it through unspoilt mixed woodland and continue, ignoring any turnings off, along what can be a very muddy track, especially in winter.

Sometime later, you will pass over a stream after which you should continue ahead, now going uphill. The Obelisk Pond will soon come into view on your left. You should continue straight on through rhodedendron bushes, ignoring a track off to the right signposted to "Parkside Nursery Cottage". You will soon arrive at the car park which was our starting point.

Rather than leave immediately, I recommend a drink in the Savill Garden Restaurant, which has lovely views over the gardens and allows you time to mull over the beauty and condensed history through which you have passed.

ACCOMMODATION

Aurora Garden Hotel, Windsor. Tel. 0753 868686
Approximately three miles from the walk, this is a small cosy hotel close to the town centre, but set back from the crowds. It is close to The Long Walk which enables you to join Windsor Great Walk without the need to drive. The Clematis Room Restaurant is something special with views over a unique water garden.

B&B, Old Windsor. Tel. 0753 865606
Approximately two and a half miles from the walk, accommodation is in an attractive character house which has a large well kept garden.

Youth Hostel, Windsor YHA, Windsor. Tel. 0753 861710
Approximately four miles from the walk, this hostel is in an attractive Queen Anne house in the village of Clewer (one mile west of Windsor). Accommodation is comfortable and the hostel is licenced to sell alcohol with meals. It can get very crowded in summer, so book ahead.

Camping & Caravanning, Hurley Caravan & Camping Park, Hurley. Tel. 0628 823501
Approximately twelve miles from the walk, this is a large but pleasant site on the south bank of the river Thames. It has all the main facilities and although it can become crowded, the owners are careful to ensure that pitches are a good distance apart.

N.B. There is a wealth of accommodation in and around Windsor. For a complete list, write to the Tourist & Information Centre, Windsor and Eaton Central Station, Windsor, Berkshire (Tel. 0753 852010).

THE WATER CHASE

Distance: 8 miles (12.75 km)
Time: Allow approximately 4½ hours
Map: Ordnance Survey Landranger Map 174

THE WATER CHASE
BERKSHIRE

START
KINTBURY
HIGH STREET
105M

HAMSTEAD
MARSHALL
100M

FINISH
KINTBURY
HIGH STREET
105M

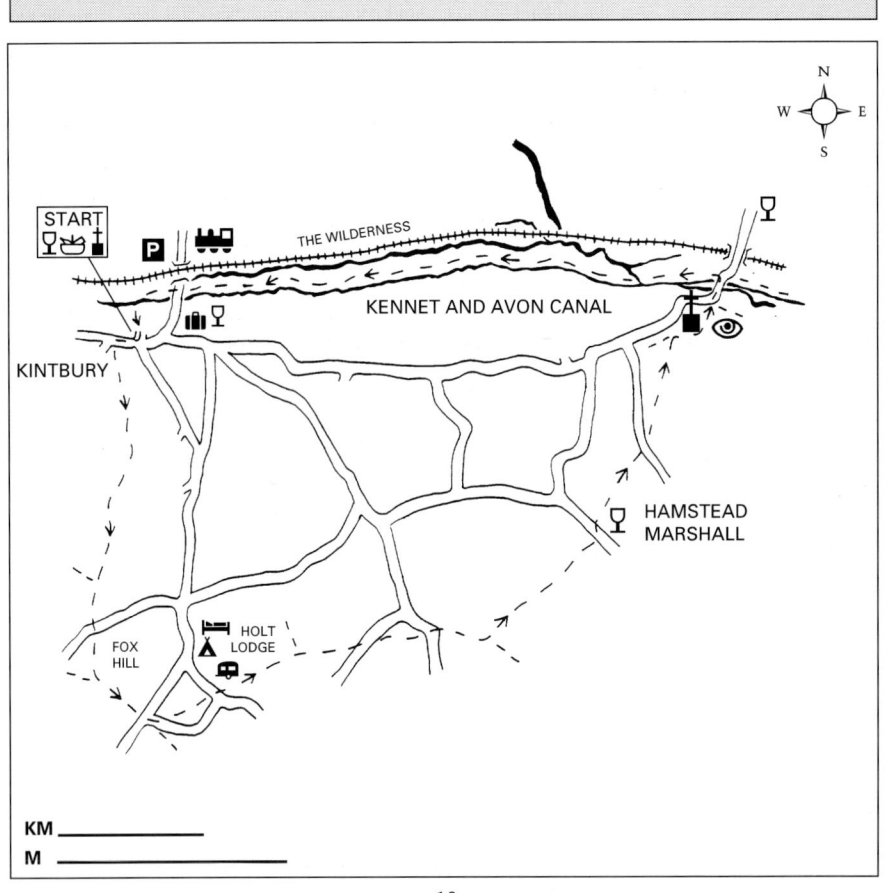

WALK SUMMARY

This is a pleasant and relatively short walk, a good graduation if you are an inexperienced walker, from Windsor Great Walk (see page 1). Starting from Kintbury on the banks of the Kennet and Avon canal, your route takes you through some of the quieter countryside of the Kennet valley with the final stretch along the canal tow path. You are close to water throughout the walk and cross several streams, tributaries of the river Kennet. The going is easy throughout, though there are in places, streams to cross without bridges and at the time of writing, two fences minus their stiles. This is often the price you have to pay when exploring lesser used paths but, in return, the countryside through which you pass is unspoilt and comes with all the benefits that that brings.

START - OS. 384668 Map 174)

The walk starts from Kintbury Post Office (The Corner Stores), which is located at a crossroads linking Inkpen and Church streets with the High Street. If coming by car, the easiest way to get there is to take the A4 between Hungerford and Newbury. Three miles east of Hungerford, take a road south signposted to Kintbury. As a guide, this is opposite a road signposted to Wickham. Follow the road to go over a railway line and the canal and continue to reach Kintbury village centre. Street parking is possible in the village, however it is advisable to park your car at the public car park beside the canal. This walk also has the added advantage of starting at a village with a railway station and the village station, Kintbury, is relatively well served. There is no obvious alternative start.

THE WATER CHASE

Kintbury is a village worth exploring though this is probably better done at the end of the walk.

Kintbury (OS. 384668 Map 174) *had existed for centuries before the coming of the canal and railway which brought it fame and fortune, first as an important commercial centre and later as a tourist attraction. The first known settlers here were the Saxons, though before them the Romans had a fairly large settlement on nearby Irish Hill. It was the Saxons however, who gave Kintbury its name, Kintbury being derived from the Saxon "Cynetanbrig", meaning "fortress on the Kennet". That Kintbury was a Saxon fortress is not surprising for it lay on the long disputed border of the Saxon kingdoms of Mercia and Wessex. Years later, it would have seen more bloodshed when in the 10th century, Viking invaders sailed up the Thames to Reading and launched their attack against what we now call Berkshire. It is probably for this reason that a large Saxon burial place was discovered here and that the Saxons regarded Kintbury as a holy place.*

With the coming of the Normans, Kintbury settled down to a more secure future and the main industries were established, most of which centred around the three mills on the river Kennet. In 1267, Kintbury's importance grew when it was granted the right to hold a weekly market and two fairs each year. In the Middle Ages, such rights were jealously fought over as they brought prosperity to a town. Kintbury was no exception and became more powerful than its larger neighbour, Hungerford.

In 1810, the canal through the village was opened and the easier transportation brought new industry such as the manufacture of whiting, silk milling, watercress farming and later even iron working. Kintbury's main source of income however, continued to come from agriculture controlled by several large manors which encircled the village. The coming of the industrial revolution brought steam mechanisation to the farms and work, in particular threshing, previously done by manual labour, could now be done by machine. Thomas Hardy gives a vivid description of a steam threshing machine in his tragic tale, "Tess of the D'Urbevilles".

Apart from the lower cost and improved efficiency of mechanisation, landowners throughout the south were relieved to sack their manual labourers, many of whom were beginning to show dissent after years of suffering low wages whilst the old Corn Laws had kept food prices high. In 1830, the tensions which had been gradually mounting finally surfaced and farm labourers across the south united in revolt under the dubious leadership of one Captain Swing. The revolt was particularly strong at Kintbury and became so serious that a detachment of Grenadier guards was sent from London to quell the trouble. Their arrival meant a quick end to the riots and nearly one hundred men were arrested, most of them in "The Blue Ball" pub which had been used as their headquarters. The ringleader at Kintbury, William Winterbourne, was hanged. His followers were deported to Australia. Winterbourne's grave was recently rediscovered on the south west side of the church yard.

As already mentioned, I recommend you take time to explore Kintbury at the end of your walk. With this in mind, I have purposely kept back a few tales of the church, the canal and Kintbury's ghosts, to recall on your return to the village.

From the Post Office walk up, or west, along Kintbury's long High Street and pass "The Blue Ball" pub, Courage, after which you should turn left along a private lane, Titcomb Way. This is signposted as a public footpath. The lane soon bends left and you should leave it here to continue straight on along a narrow footpath between fences. When the fences end, pass through the remains of an old kissing gate and carry straight on along the path which now runs between fields. The views ahead in the distance are of the daunting Inkpen Beacon and Walbury Hill.

As you progress, the footpath becomes quite thickly hedged and then leads to a stile which you should cross into a field. Follow the right hand perimeter of the field round, where there is a stream on your right and continue as the path narrows and runs between the stream on your right and a fenced field on your left. Stay on the path to soon cross the stream by way of a wooden footbridge into a field. Once in the field, carry straight on along the left hand perimeter and at the far left hand corner, go over a stile into the next field. Cross the centre of the field bearing just slightly diagonally right, following a line of trees on your right and heading for a house in view, "Titcomb Manor", one of seven manor houses around Kintbury which are recorded in the Domesday Book. Just before the house and on reaching the far side of the field, bear left along a grass track to follow the field perimeter in the direction of a footpath sign.

Follow the track as it bends right and pass through a metal gate onto a lane. Turn left along the lane, pass over a small stream and shortly after, ignore a signposted footpath off to the left to continue past a house. Stay on the lane until it bends left and here leave it to carry straight on over a stile into a field. This is signposted as a public footpath. Do not make the mistake of turning right along a track to "Titcomb Farm", also signposted as a footpath.

Go straight across the field along the right hand perimeter and at the far side pass through a gap in the hedgerow (there was obviously once a gate here which may be reinstated in the future) and continue ahead along the right hand perimeter of the next field making for some houses in the distance. At the far right hand corner, cross

12

a stile to follow a fenced footpath between gardens to meet a lane. Cross the lane, go over a stile at the other side and continue ahead along another fenced and signposted public footpath. This runs initially behind a house and thereafter between fields.

The path later comes out to an open grass area in front of a house at Fox Hill. Bear left here and cross the centre of the grass area with fencing on your left and the house on your right. Pass through a gap in a hedge to join a small footpath in front of another house and turn right along the path which runs between holly bushes and laurels. This leads out onto a gravel drive belonging to the house on your left, "Jangles". Go across the drive and follow a track downhill through woodland and at the bottom cross a small stream to continue ahead along a path the other side which joins the drive to "Willow Farm", now visible on your left.

Once on the drive, continue ahead and on meeting a second drive way, again carry straight on. The drive passes two more picturesque cottages, "Bridle Path Cottage" and "Tubbs Cottage", before arriving at a lane beside a bungalow. Ahead of you now should you wish to take a detour is Inkpen Common, protected by BBONT, Berkshire, Buckinghamshire and Oxfordshire Naturalist Trust. Our route however, is across the lane to follow another lane ahead where after a short distance, you will pass "Peartree Cottage" on the left. Immediately after this, turn left onto a signposted public footpath which runs between hedges. After approximately twenty metres, go over a stile into a field.

Go straight across the field in the direction of the public footpath sign and at the far side, cross over two stiles to enter another field. This time, go gently diagonally right across the field, again in the direction of the public footpath sign and on reaching the field perimeter cross two further stiles. Thereafter, turn immediately left and follow the left hand perimeter of the next field.

After passing some farm buildings and a house on your left, you will reach the far corner of the field and a stile which you should cross onto a lane. To your left here is the entrance to "Holt Lodge" (recommended accommodation). Turn right along the lane and after approximately twenty metres, go over a stile on your left to join a signposted public footpath. The footpath continues ahead along the left hand perimeter of a field, lined by a number of proud oaks. Once across the field, pass behind "Holt Lodge Farm" and ignore a grass fenced track running in the same direction. You should ensure you continue along the field perimeter and pass to the rear of the walled garden belonging to "Holt Lodge" and thereafter, an orchard.

At the far corner of the field, pass through a metal gate and do not be tempted to cross a stile into a field on your left. If you take time to have a breather here, the views behind now are of Walbury Hill and you can take comfort in the knowledge that for today anyway, the hill is not part of the itinerary. Continue ahead along the left hand perimeter of the next field and when the fencing on your left ends go straight on across the centre of the field. At the field end, cross a stile into another field, where once again you should follow the left hand perimeter ahead. After a short distance, when the field perimeter bends left, you should ignore a signposted footpath left and continue across the field, bearing gently right. As a guide, you should head for a footpath sign ahead to your right in the distance, which is just to the right of a house directly ahead.

The field is larger than most and usually of grass. As you cross, look out for patches of flattened grass often with a scattering of what looks like rabbit droppings. These in *i* fact, belong to the brown hare (see also "The Hungerford Hare"). The patches of flattened grass are called "forms" and are made by the hare to hide its young until they are old enough to run with the mother. A separate form is made for each of the litter which normally numbers about three. If you are very lucky you may even find an occupied form (so watch where you tread!), but if you do, take care not to disturb it as the mother may abandon her young.

On meeting the footpath sign at the far side, pass through a gate onto a lane. (The gate, at the time of writing, is temporary and could well be replaced with a stile in future). Turn left along the lane to reach the house mentioned earlier **(OS. 398648)**. Behind it is a copse with the odd name, Skew-Whiff, which must hold a story. Opposite the house, look out for a signposted public footpath. Take this to immediately jump across a small stream, at this stage the youthful river Enborne *i* which runs for several miles, much of its journey forming the boundary between Berkshire and Hampshire. It eventually joins the river Kennet at Woolhampton. In the early part of this century, there were plans to dam the Enborne to provide a water supply for London. If this plan had materialised, we could currently be standing under several feet of water. If you are walking this way in summer and I tell you that jumping the stream is difficult, you would laugh in my face, for the jump is merely a step as the stream can dry to a trickle. In winter or wet weather however, it is a different matter and an energetic leap is called for. If athletics are not your forte then be prepared to get your feet wet!

After the stream another obstacle presents itself, this time a fence with no stile. The fence however, is one of strong wooden rails and easy to negotiate. Once over, you will find yourself in a small field which you should cross, bearing diagonally left. At the far side, go over the fence again and cross the Enborne once more, a second chance to get your feet wet. Thereafter, go over a stile into the next field and cross the centre of this field, heading for a farm gate and stile the other side. To your right now, as a guide, is "Holt Manor Farm".

Go over the stile and turn right along a lane for approximately fifteen paces and then leave it turning left onto a track which runs between fields. The track soon follows the perimeter of a wood on your right and later bends right towards the picturesque "Watermans Farm". You should leave the track here and turn left in the direction of the public footpath sign. Do not take the footpath bearing right which leads directly across the field, but take the one bearing left. As you enter the field, the sign actually points across the field. However, as the farmer has taken the trouble to leave access, I recommend you follow the grass track along the left hand perimeter. On reaching the field corner and the edge of some woodland, turn right to continue along the track, still following the left hand field perimeter. On your right in the distance, is the distinct outline of Beacon Hill.

On reaching the next field corner you will meet some wooden railings on your left. Climb over these (there was once a stile here which will hopefully be replaced in the future), and follow a path ahead through brambles. After approximately ten paces, you will meet a junction of paths and tracks. Go straight across a track and follow a narrow footpath ahead through the unspoilt deciduous woodland of Great Holt Copse. Stay on the path ignoring any turnings off, to eventually reach a stile. Cross this into a field and continue across the field, bearing diagonally right in the direction of the footpath sign. On reaching the crest of the hill, look out for a farm gate ahead in front of "Plumb Farm", for which you should head. There are excellent views here over the Kennet valley and beyond the farm, to the hamlet of Hamstead Marshall, our next destination.

Pass through the farm gate onto a farm track and carry straight on. As you near "Plumb Farm" you will probably be greeted by a chorus of barking, as the farm also doubles as a kennels and the headquarters of the National Canine Defence League. The residents are usually very excited at the sight or sound of any passing walker who is viewed, I am sure, as lunch! As you reach the farm, the track becomes a tarmac drive and you should continue to follow it to soon arrive at a road and the hamlet of Hamstead Marshall. The name is derived from a Norman landlord, Gilbert the Marshall, who was Marshall at the Court of Henry I. Opposite and very convenient, is "The White Hart Inn", a free house which also has a restaurant.

Turn left along the road for approximately thirty metres until you are opposite the Elm Farm Research Centre, and turn right onto a public bridleway, passing through a metal farm gate onto a track. The track which can be very muddy, leads between farm buildings before passing between fields. At the far side, stay on the track to pass through a gap in the hedge and continue across the next field. Approximately half way across the field, the track passes through an area which at times can be flooded. To avoid this, there is a small footpath just to the left of the track specifically for walkers. To your left here also, is a small pond which with its many rotting trees and melancholy reflections, looks the perfect setting for a local ghost story.

Follow the track to the far side of the field and exit by way of a metal gate to arrive at a lane. Cross the lane and join a signposted footpath the other side, passing through a kissing gate. The footpath winds uphill through grasses and brambles and can at times be undefined. There is a prominent path off to the left leading to a clump of beech trees which you should ignore. Our route remains on the footpath, running through an open area between the beech trees on the left and some oak trees on your right. It eventually meets a stile between banks.

Go over the stile and carry straight on across a field, where the fencing on your right marks the border of "Edgecombe Nursing Home", once "Hamstead Park". The way across the field is undefined. You should therefore, make for four pillars ahead in the distance, which are the remains of the old gateways to "Hamstead Park". Half way across the field you will pass a man-made pond on your left, after which you will gain your best views right to "Edgecombe Nursing Home". Continue to the far side of the field and do not make the mistake of heading for the far corner where there is a metal gate, to exit by way of a temporary gate constructed of barbed wire and posts situated slightly to the left of the field corner.

Go straight across the next field where the way is again very undefined and head for a church the other side. You now pass close to the old gate pillars which guide your way across the field. They stand in eerie isolation, the driveways which they once guarded having been lost long ago through neglect. The pillars however, despite the burgeoning grass residing in the many cracks and the crumbling of ageing plaster, still retain an elegance in testimony to the once great house they served.

Hamstead Park (OS. 424660 Map 174) *was a manor of some importance as far back as the Domesday survey in the 11th century. With the ascension of Henry I to the throne in 1100, the manor became the official residence of the Marshall to the Crown. The most famous of these was William the Marshall, Earl of Pembroke, who served Henry III. The office of Marshall was separated from the manor during the* reign of Edward I. However, it remained one of the more important manors in the country and two centuries later, was a favourite of Richard III who was a frequent visitor to the hunting lodge in the grounds. In 1620, the manor was bought by William Craven, later knighted by Charles I to become the first Earl of Craven.

Sir William Craven who already had a house, "Ashdown Park" (N.T.) near Lambourn, set about building a second house here at Hamstead, modelled it is said, on the famous Heidelberg Castle. It is a matter of debate whether the house was intended for his close friend, Queen Elizabeth of Bohemia, but as she died in 1662 before the house was started, it is more probable that it was modelled on Heidelberg in her memory. The Dutch architect, Sir Balthazerger Gerbier, was employed to design the house and forced to come out of retirement after several of his other business activities had failed. The project was to be his last and he died before he had the chance to see his work completed. Sadly, we cannot see it either, as the house was destroyed by fire in 1718, leaving only the gateways and some of the park wall.

It is ironic that the house should be destroyed by fire as Sir William was well known for his efforts in fighting the great fire of London, after which fire fighting became his hobby. The destruction of the house was one of several tragedies to dog the Craven family. Much of their misfortune it is said, was due to a gypsy curse several hundred years ago. Common to the time, the curse foretold the early death of Craven's male descendants until the Craven name no longer existed. Undeterred by the curse or the fire, the Craven's built a new house and continued to live here surrounded by the magnificent seven hundred acre park until 1984, when they were forced to sell the estate, which has now become a nursing home.

Pass the lone gate pillars and at the far side of the field cross over a stile and continue to reach the perimeter of the church yard.

St. Mary's Church (OS. 420667 Map 174) was here long before Sir William built his own Heidelberg Castle. In fact, the church was originally Norman, though successive heavy-handed restorations, first in the 14th century and again in the 19th century, have left this period virtually unrecognisable.

Inside, a series of box pews along with a fine Jacobean pulpit, preserve some of the original character of the church, though the door is normally locked and it is doubtful that you will have the opportunity to experience this. Do not be too disheartened, for the church's greatest asset is its position. Sitting on a ridge above the Kennet valley, fine views are to be had from the northern side of the church yard. The glorious sight of the meandering River Kennet and

A lock on the Kennet & Avon Canal

the canal cutting a more direct route through hazy water meadows, more than compensate for missing a few box pews. Another gem not locked away, is an impressive mausoleum housing the Craven family vault, situated at the eastern end of the church yard. It is almost completely hidden, quite a feat when you see its size.

To continue our route, turn right in front of the church yard and follow a grass track which leads gently away from the walled church perimeter into a field. After a short distance, the track bears gently left to lead downhill through parkland. On your left you will pass two mounds, part of the remains of the old house and on your right, a pond, which I assume is all that remains of the original moat. Soon after, the track forks and you should take the left hand fork to continue between an avenue of trees.

At a "T" junction, cross a drive and go over a stile ahead onto a lane. Turn right along the lane to pass "Hamstead Mill" (now converted into luxury apartments) on your right and thereafter, cross the River Kennet. This is a particularly picturesque spot and worth stopping to enjoy. Continue to go over a second bridge across the Kennett and Avon canal and immediately after, turn left to join the canal tow path. If however, all this water is making you thirsty, a short detour (half a mile there and back) along the road ahead will bring you to an attractive thatched pub, "The Water Rat", at Marsh Benham. This, in my opinion, is the best pub on the route and worth the detour. In summer, you can enjoy a rest in a pleasant sloping garden whilst puzzling over the need for the seven chimneys which rise out of the thatch. Inside, the walls have been tastefully painted with pastel country scenes based around animals. Perhaps best of all though, is the pub's selection of real ales and the adventurous menu.

Returning to the tow path, you will immediately pass Hamstead Lock. Locks have always held a certain fascination for me and I can easily sit for hours watching their operation. This can also be cruelly amusing when they are worked by an unsuspecting crew on their first canal holiday. Please remember though that despite their harmless appearance, locks can be extremely dangerous. To learn the history of the canal please refer to "The Hungerford Hare".

After the lock, the canal enters a delightful world of lazy water meadows nestling between soft green hillsides and friendly woodland. Occasionally, you will pass pill boxes left over from the Second World War, a second line of defence should the southern counties have fallen. Soon after the first of these, you can say your final farewell to St. Mary's church, which sits majestically on a ridge to your left. Eventually, the tow path takes you over the river Kennet once more, by way of a metal bridge to meet your second lock, Copse Lock. Just before the lock, the river and canal merge to become one for a short distance, before the river continues on its own course to power "Hamstead Mill".

Continue along the tow path through more unspoilt countryside to reach the next lock, Dreweat's Lock, which has a typical canal bridge from which you can enjoy a few tranquil moments and take in the beauty of your surroundings. Just before the bridge, the canal has been widened to form a "winding place", where boats can turn around. Feeding the winding place is Peartree Brook, one of the many streams rising below the escarpment of the North Hampshire Downs.

After Dreweat's Lock, the canal runs between Irish Hill to the south and an area of wooded marsh, appropriately called The Wilderness, to the north. The pleasant wooded slopes of Irish Hill hide a huge chalk quarry which supplied chalk to a number of mills along the river producing the powder used in the manufacture of whitewash. Search amongst the undergrowth at the base of the hill and you will find some of the old workings of these mills which were simply abandoned to nature. Protected by Irish Hill and The Wilderness, this part of the canal is one of the best places to see the wildlife common to the Kennet valley.

Wildlife in the Kennet Valley. *Apart from the ever hungry ducks, the waterways provide a habitat for a wide variety of birds. Those that are easily spotted include the mute swan, the Canadian goose, the coote and the shy moorhen which stays close to the bank, forever ready to dart for cover. Equally common but less easy to spot, are the grey heron and the kingfisher, the latter normally only seen as a dazzling flash as it skims the water in search of food. If you are lucky, you may even see a cormorant. These are usually coastal birds but occasionally come inland in search of fresh water fish. The cormorant will normally be seen sitting on an overhanging branch, its neck stretched high whilst it digests its meal. In summer, the air above the canal is filled with the acrobatics of swallows, swifts and house martins, as they catch insects on the wing. The rich meadows and woods which cover the valley floor also provide a habitat for a great variety of birds, too numerous to name here. To avoid the frustration of spotting a species you do not recognise, I suggest you invest in a pocket book on birds.*

In the deep waters of the canal, there is perhaps the most ferocious of our fresh water fish, the pike. The pike which feeds on small fish, can also find your toes attractive, so think twice before you cool those feet in the canal! You will have to be particularly alert if you want to spot a pike as they normally stay very still lying in wait for an unsuspecting fish (or walker's toes) to provide the next meal.

Three mammals which inhabit the banks of the river and canal are the water shrew, the water vole and the mink. The water shrew is distinguishable by its black coat and white underbody. It feeds mainly on worms and small spiders but will take to the water to catch fish or even frogs. The water vole is much larger and has a brown coat. Its appearance means it is often mistaken for a rat and is commonly called a water rat. Unlike the water shrew, the water vole feeds almost entirely on waterside plants. Much rarer but growing in population is the mink, which is now considered a naturalised British inhabitant. Minks were first introduced to Britain from North America in the 1920's for the fur trade. The naturalised minks today are the descendents of some of the luckier arrivals who escaped from the fur farms. They are particularly good swimmers and fish forms a large part of their staple diet. The Kennet valley is an ideal habitat for the mink which never lives far from water, so keep your eye peeled.

Two past inhabitants of the valley which sadly you will not see today, are the otter and the beaver. Evidence of beaver dams have been found in the valley, particularly near Hamstead and up until the 10th century, an island on the river Kennet near Brimpton was referred to as Beaver Island. The otter lasted longer but this too disappeared, mainly as a result of modern farming methods.

I have only touched on the first chapter of which there are many on the wildlife to be found in and around the Kennet valley. For example, I have not mentioned frogs, toads and snakes, nor the wealth of insect life such as the glamorous dragon and damsel flies which create such a regal display above the water. The rest must be down to you to discover.
Tread carefully and keep your senses about you and you will be rewarded by a display missed by many who use the tow path. If you are particularly keen to see more, time your walk to pass this way at dawn or dusk.

The canal leaves Irish Hill and later passes under Shepherds Bridge, though it is unlikely that you will see sheep crossing it today. After Shepherds Bridge it is only three quarters of a mile to Kintbury. Kintbury is approached by crossing a small concrete bridge over an arm of the river Kennet beside a white cottage. Just after the cottage, you will see Kintbury railway station on your right. Here, the canal forks with one arm going to "Kintbury Mill" and the other to Kintbury Lock, ahead. You should continue to meet a lane at a bridge just prior to the lock where on your left, there is the temptation of a stop at "The Dundas Arms Hotel", a Morland inn. This spot is a popular place for tourists and weekend visitors - so expect to be greeted by crowds!

Cross the lane and continue along the tow path the other side passing Kintbury Lock. Today this part of the canal, Kintbury Wharf, is heavy with pleasure boats. It was a very different story years ago when Kintbury Wharf was the hub of industry at Kintbury.

Kintbury Wharf (OS. 386671 Map 174) *even with its pleasure boats and holiday trade, is a fraction of what it was only one hundred years ago. Then the wharf unloaded a steady flow of iron and coke from South Wales for the iron works. Watercress went daily to London, whiting from the mills to Bristol and timber to Reading. The large mill on the far bank ground flour and corn was brought by barge along the head-race (a channel running parallel with the canal on the far bank), where it was unloaded. This practice only stopped in 1960 when the mill closed. It has now been converted into luxury apartments.*

"The Dundas Arms Hotel", is named after Charles Dundas, Chairman of the Kennet and Avon Canal Project for forty years. The hotel itself does not rely entirely upon its advantageous position to guarantee custom. Apart from serving the reliable Morland ales, it has a pleasant restaurant which takes advantage of local produce, in particular fish, to provide a tempting menu. All this is backed up by an extensive wine cellar. If you prefer the simpler things in life, the hotel serves some keenly priced bar meals.

On meeting another bridge, bear right and follow a path uphill onto the bridge and then turn left to go over it and the canal itself. You will now follow a tarmac path heading into Kintbury which soon leads out to a driveway. On your right here is

"The Old Vicarage", a stately Victorian house (recommended accommodation). Cross the drive way and continue along a stepped footpath ahead to enter the church yard of St. Mary's. Here the path forks and I suggest you take the left hand fork, thereby allowing you to visit the church itself en route.

St. Mary's, Kintbury (OS. 383669 Map 174) *is of Norman origin, but as with so many other churches in Berkshire, has been heavily restored. Today, only the sturdy tower which was built in 1200 and added to in the 15th century along with the south and west doorways, remain as monuments to the original builders. The church tower forms part of the legend of the Kintbury Great Bell. This tells of how during a great storm, part of the tower collapsed and a bell subsequently fell into the river. A wizard gave instructions to pass a chain through a hook attached to the bell and after this, twelve white heifers led by twelve maidens in white robes tied with red sashes, were to pull the chain and then only by the light of the moon. Nobody was to speak, instructed the wizard, or the chain would break. The bell had almost been recovered when the Kintbury witch cried out, "Here comes the great Kintbury bell, in spite of all the devils in Hell!". The chain broke and the bell was lost to the waters of the Kennet.*

Apart from the legend, the church is connected with two local ghosts. The first is Mary Dexter whose tomb can be found in the church yard. Her husband died in India and unable to be buried beside him, on her death she asked for her husband's sword to be buried with her. If you pass through the church yard after dark, it is said that you can hear the sword rattling in her coffin. The second is a man with a hat and a long black cloak who has been seen sitting in the front pew of the church.

If the ghosts do not put you off, a visit to the church is very worthwhile. On the walls there are almost thirty mural tablets. Included in these, is one to Charles Dundas and another to one of the Craven family at Hamstead. There is also a memorial to Mary Dexter and her husband.

Follow the path away from the church and exit via the main gate. Carry straight on along Church Lane, lined by cottages, to arrive at the High Street at Kintbury and our starting point. To help recover after the walk, apart from "The Blue Ball" and "The Dundas Arms", Kintbury has a third pub in the form of "The Prince of Wales". If alcohol will only kill you off, there is a cafe in Church Lane and a small yard, Thatchers Yard, which has a number of unusual shops. Whatever your choice, do not rush home, but have a well deserved rest by slowly discovering the delights of this canalside village.

ACCOMMODATION

The Dundas Arms Hotel, Kintbury. Tel: 0488 58263
On the walk. I have already enthused on the delights on this two hundred year old inn. Now you can crown a wonderful day by staying in one of the rooms converted from the stable block overlooking the canal. No need to tramp up the tow path in search of wildlife here, simply draw back your curtains.

The Old Vicarage, Kintbury. Tel: 0488 58073
On the walk, this is a beautiful place to stay. The house which is one of the most elegant in Kintbury, sits on the bank of the canal in a wonderfully secluded position.

Holt Lodge, Nr. Kintbury. Tel: 04884 244
On the walk, this is the ideal place if you want complete rest and relaxation. Several miles from Kintbury itself, accommodation is in a pretty Queen Anne house, surrounded by open farmland. Holt Lodge also runs a small campsite with facilities for caravans.

Youth Hostel, The Court Hill Ridgeway Centre YHA. Tel: 02357 60253
Approximately twelve miles from the walk, this is a purpose built hostel from the reconstruction of four barns. The hostel is in a beautiful position with views over the Vale of the White Horse. The grounds include a wood where you can camp and has a barbecue area.

Camping Skiffs (London Office). Tel: 081 941 4858
For a taste of the past and something unusual why not try a camping skiff. This is a long wooden rowing boat which has a removable canvas cover to convert the boat into a tent at night.

ROMANS REVENGE

Distance: 10¼ miles (16.5 km)
Time: Allow approximately 5½ hours
Map: Ordnance Survey Landranger Map 175

ROMANS REVENGE
BERKSHIRE

START	KILN POND	CALLEVA	FINISH
STRATFIELD	80M	ATREBATUM	STRATFIELD
MORTIMER		95M	MORTIMER
55M			55M

PADWORTH COMMON
MORTIMER WEST END
BENYONS ENCLOSURE
AMPHITHEATRE
START
STRATFIELD MORTIMER
SILCHESTER
CALLEVA ATREBATUM
FOWDRY BROOK

KM
M

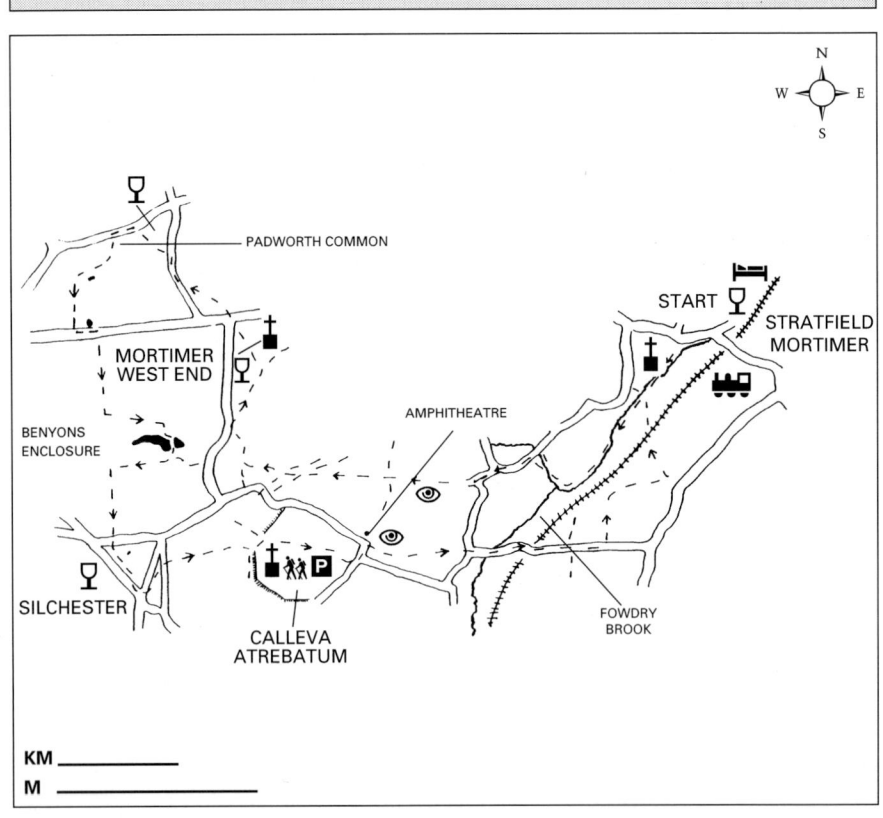

22

Walk Summary

This is a pleasant walk along the quieter paths of Berkshire and North Hampshire. The accompanying scenery is one of tranquil rolling farm land divided by clear water streams and shady woodland. Along the way you will encounter many pleasant surprises, including two welcome pubs. However, the definite highlight is the deserted Roman town of Calleva Atrebatum. The going is easy with plenty to occupy your mind. Some of the paths can be muddy, but to compensate there are no steep ascents.

Start - OS. 669641 Map 175

The walk starts from the church at Stratfield Mortimer. By car, if coming from the south, take the A33 from Basingstoke heading for Reading and at the roundabout just before the M4, turn left following the signs to Burghfield and Stratfield Mortimer. Follow the road to Mortimer where on entering the village you will arrive at a "T" junction. Turn right, pass "The Railway Inn" and soon after, you will see the village church on your left. There is a parking area in front of the church, but if there is a service taking place road parking nearby is fairly easy, though as always, please consider the local residents.

If coming from any other direction, it is best to make for junction 11 on the M4 and from there take the A33 south, signposted to Basingstoke. At the first roundabout, turn right signposted to Burghfield and Stratfield Mortimer and follow the directions given above.

The nearest railway station is at Mortimer. From there it is only a five minute walk to reach Stratfield Mortimer church. An alternative start can be made from St. Mary's church within the Roman walls of Calleva, where there is a small car park (OS. 643624).

ROMANS REVENGE

The walk starts from the drive leading to the church at Stratfield Mortimer, signposted as a byway.

Stratfield Mortimer (OS. 669641 Map 175). *There is little to tell of Stratfield Mortimer itself. The name is derived from "strata" Roman for "street" and Stratfield literally means an area of open land crossed by a Roman road. Mortimer originates from the Norman Lord of the Manor, Ralf Mortimer. Apart from the church, there are several buildings lining the village street which catch the eye, the two most noticeable at the start are "The Railway Inn", Whitbread, and an unusual garage called "Just Beetles", which specialises in the Volkswagen Beetle.*

The church is Victorian and was built in 1869 on the site of an earlier church. Inside, there is a rare Saxon tombstone which was found buried under the old tower. It is dated 994 AD and the inscription reads,

> "On the 8th before the Kalends of October Aegalward
> son of Kypping was laid in this place
> Blessed be he who prays for his soul
> Toki wrote me"

Toki was Courtier to King Cnute and Kypping, Lord of the Manor at Mortimer. Aegalward was a well known Saxon mentioned in the Chronicle of 994 AD, an historian, translator and an Ealdorman (Governor of Hampshire). It would appear that Aegalward must have befriended the invading Danes to have such a memorial errected, though in his defence peace had all but been declared when the stone was inscribed, with Cnute becoming the first Danish king of England just twentyone years later. Apart from the tombstone, the church also has an ancient font and an interesting brass.

Take the drive to the church and unless you wish to visit, continue past the main entrance passing the drive to "Ladyfield House" on your right and continue over a stream to reach a stile. Go over the stile and turn immediately right to follow the right hand perimeter of a field, where on your right in the grounds of "Ladyfield House", there is a large pond frequented by a number of rather surprisingly shy ducks.

The field perimeter gradually bears right and it is worth stopping at this point to look back and enjoy views to Stratfield Mortimer church and "Ladyfield House". Continue ahead, now following the course of the Fowdry Brook on your right, until you reach the far side of the field. Pass through a metal gate which, at the time of writing, is virtually out of use and thereafter, continue along a path slightly raised above a field on your left, still following the brook on your right. You will soon see a conveniently placed tree stump on your right where you may wish to take an early rest overlooking the brook and with luck, you may also spot one of the kingfishers which fish this part of the brook.

On reaching the far side of the field on your left, you will meet a footbridge over the brook on your right which you should take. At the other side, ignore a signposted footpath directly ahead and turn immediately left instead, to follow a well maintained path along the left hand perimeter of a field. At the far side of the field, continue straight on through a gap in the hedge, ignoring a wide wooden bridge on your left, to pass into another field. Carry straight on across the next field and half way across, look out for a stile on your left which you should go over into a narrower field. Continue straight ahead to rejoin the bank of the brook and then turn right along the left hand perimeter of the field, with the brook on your left. If you pass this way in summer your route along the brook will be lined by a mass of richly coloured foxgloves, more prominent than I have seen anywhere else. Also, growing in large clumps are the herbs borage and common comfrey.

At the far left hand corner of the field, cross over a stile and a ditch into another field, where you should continue ahead still following the course of the brook on your left. You will now cross the head of a long oblong field and it is not long before you reach the other side, where there is a stile on your left. Do not cross the stile, but turn right and follow the field perimeter heading for a cottage in the distance. You will still have water on your left albeit this time much narrower, being a tributary to the Fowdry Brook.

The field gradually narrows as you progress and further on, you should ignore a cattle crossing over the stream on your left. Carry straight on to the end of the field to reach and cross a stile and follow a narrow footpath ahead to shortly meet a lane beside a bridge, Tanhouse Bridge, on your left. There is a footpath sign with a white arrow pointing right here, marking a Berkshire County Council recreational route, part of which we have just been following. Our route from here however, is left along the lane away from the recreational route, going over the bridge and at the same time, crossing into Hampshire.

The lane climbs gently and winds between fields, hidden in the main by banks topped by thick hedgerows. In summer you are accompanied by swallows who swoop acrobatically, feeding off insects on the wing. It is a pleasant walk and although along a lane, you will be very unlucky to meet a car as the lane merely acts as a connection between a few farms and little else. It is not long before you meet the first of these farms, "Brocas Lands". Ignore a lane off to the right here and continue straight on to soon pass the farm house itself, a lovely affair with an old milk churn outside its porch.

Approximately forty metres after the farm house the lane bends sharp left. You should leave it here to carry straight on along a track (**OS 653631**). Before you do so however, it may be worth pausing here to catch your breath and enjoy the views back over the surrounding farm land. The track continues to climb gently and passes "Sheepgrove Farm" on the left across the fields and soon after, bends left. You should leave the track at this point and continue straight on to pass through two wooden posts into a field.

Go straight across the field in the direction of the public footpath sign. When I walked this way, the farmer had cut a narrow path through the wheat growing at the time - it was a lovely sensation to stop at the centre of the field, with nothing other than the bobbing heads of the wheat for company. Pass under some electricity pilons and continue to reach and cross a stile at the far side. Cross a second stile to enter the next field and continue straight on in the direction of the yellow arrow, also marked by the figure 23.

Half way across the field pass through a line of trees, once part of the field boundary and continue to the far side where you should cross a stile into another field. Cross the field, bearing right heading for the far right hand corner. Go over a stile constructed from wooden rails beside a gate, into a field on your right and walk diagonally left across this field heading for the far corner. As a guide, there is a farm ahead to your left as you cross the field and also on your left, you can see the white stone walls of the ancient Roman town of Calleva, through which we will pass on our return journey. Also in the field, look out for the rings in the grass which are in fact mushroom rings, once thought to be the work of fairies.

At the far corner of the field go over a stile, again made from wooden rails and cross a farm track and then a second stile into a small field. Continue straight on along the right hand field perimeter and at the far side, cross another stile into the next field. Ignore a gate on your right and carry straight on, again following the right hand perimeter, and after approximately twenty metres, look out for a well hidden footpath which leaves the field through a gap in the hedge on the right.

The initial going can be quite tough, but it is not long before the path becomes more prominent, being lined by trees. After a short distance, you will meet a "T" junction in the form of a grass track, where you should turn right. If you are walking this way in summer, you will be met by the pleasant sweet smell of wild honeysuckle which hangs in places from the trees on either side.

The track quickly descends becoming muddier as you progress and at the bottom of a valley crosses a small bridge over a stream, much visited in summer by vibrant blue and green damselflies. It then soon meets a lane where you should turn right for approximately thirty paces and right again onto a track signposted as a right of way. As a guide, this is just in front of two red brick cottages. You may however, wish to delay your walk and continue along the lane for a short distance to visit the welcoming "Red Lion Inn", a free house which has an interesting pub sign with rats painted around a pole. The pub has a comfortable interior with old beams and outside, a paved garden should you wish to enjoy the summer sun. It serves an excellent range of real ales and offers a good varied menu. If you take a break here, you will have to retrace your steps to continue our walk.

Follow the track which runs gently uphill and after passing a house on your right, take time to enjoy the views which open out on the same side across a shallow valley. Stay on the track until you eventually meet a crossing track, where you should turn left heading for the houses of Mortimer Westend. You will enter the village by passing the cricket field on your left - in summer if a game is in progress, this is a lovely spot for a short rest, especially if that last pint at the "Red Lion Inn" has gone straight to your legs!

i

The track continues to later meet a lane, just before which notice the hedge on the right bordering the track, made up of one of the biggest assortment of trees and shrubs I have come across. Turn right along the lane to meet a "T" junction. The road ahead signposted as Chapel Road, is known locally by its much older name, Welshmans Road. The name stems from the Welsh drovers who once used the road to drive their flocks to the larger markets. Cross Chapel Road and continue straight ahead, passing through a gap in some fencing to enter woodland, Stockwells Piece. Continue ahead along a wide path which runs diagonally left through the wood in the direction of a footpath sign. The wood is made up almost entirely of pines, a welcome change after the open farm land traversed so far. It is beautiful at any time of the year but in summer is particularly special, when the dark canopy of the trees is complimented by the lush green of the thick ferns growing on the woodland floor.

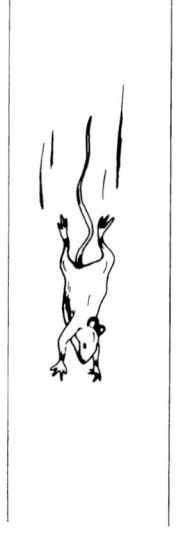

A rat on the pole at the Red Lion

As you progress, ignore another track off to the right and continue ahead to eventually meet a lane. Turn right along the lane where if you wish to avoid lane walking, you can follow a track on the right which runs parallel to your route. The lane takes you through the centre of the wood where you should look out for a footpath sign on your left sometime later (if you are following the track to the right of the lane, then you should take extra care not to miss this). Join the footpath left and continue through the wood, this time mainly deciduous and much changed from the prominent pines referred to earlier. After a short distance, you will meet a field on your right, the perimeter of which your route follows. Thereafter, stay on the footpath to cross a stream via a wooden plank bridge, which in summer is guarded by a colourful array of foxgloves.

After the bridge, the footpath soon meets a drive which you should join to carry straight on, passing between some attractive properties. As you reach the front of the properties, ignore a gravel drive left and continue straight on to meet a road (**OS. 626649**). Our way is left here. However, if you are in dire need of some more refreshment, a short detour right along the lane will bring you to "The Round Oak", Whethered. Half a mile further on from the pub (not part of our route), is a road junction known as Gibbet Piece. The name remembers the hanging in 1787 of two youths who were found guilty of murdering William Billimore. The hanging attracted ten thousand people.

Returning to our route, as instructed, turn left along the road for approximately twenty metres to reach another gravel drive (the entrance to "Manor House"), on your left. Cross the drive to take a signposted public footpath the other side. The footpath leads through a small copse and after a very short distance, arrives at a drive in front of "Birch Cottage" which has a well in its garden.

Cross the drive, the other side of which the footpath forks. You should take the right hand fork (the left hand fork simply leads to a compost heap) and follow a narrow path across Padworth Common, predominantly silver birch. Soon after, look out for a narrow footpath left (take care not to miss it), which you should follow through what I can only describe as a mini wilderness. Ignore a crossing track and continue ahead and stay on the path, which in summer can involve pushing through dense bracken, ignoring any minor turnings off. The way here can at first seem somewhat unclear. Simply keep to the more prominent path at all times and you will not get lost.

As you continue, look out for a footbridge on the left, often somewhat hidden by the leafy growth of the common, so again take care not to miss it. Go over the footbridge and cross a stile turning immediately right thereafter, in the direction of a yellow arrow also marked by the figure 1. You will now follow a rather boggy path running between open pine woodland on your left and the more dense common on the right. Continue until the pine woodland ends and then turn left to cross Burnt Common, keeping to the left of a line of telegraph poles and right of an old fence. Burnt Common is very different from the common we have just left, being mostly open grassland dotted with gorse. It is a haven for some rare plants and a variety of birds, many of which nest in the grasses, particularly the lapwings whose sounds are easily distinguished as they hover above your head in an attempt to distract you from the site of their nests.

At the second telegraph pole, you should continue ahead but ensure you are now walking to the right of the telegraph poles and not the left as before. You should still be following the old fence on your left. After passing a pond overrun with reeds on your left, Welshmans Pond, once a watering hole for the flocks of the Welsh drovers, you will come to a stile at the far side of the common, which you should cross to once again meet Welshmans Road. Turn left along the road and after a short distance, turn right onto a signposted footpath which takes the form of a track and leads directly through the centre of yet more majestic pine woodland, Benyon's Inclosure. On joining the footpath, ensure you ignore a track on the left which follows the road and soon after, another track leading off to the right.

i

The track runs through the centre of the wood where you should ignore all turnings off to the left or right. You will later meet a wide crossing track **(OS. 624635)**, where as a guide, the track you are on begins to descend immediately after this. You should turn left onto the crossing track which continues to take you through the pine wood. Sometime on, leave the track as it bends left and carry straight on in the direction of a yellow arrow which is set into one of the trees at this point. Just after, the track forks and you should take the right hand and more prominent fork which almost immediately bends right to run downhill.

As the descent becomes steeper, a narrow track joins the track you are following. You should ignore this to continue straight on, following the main track which twists before passing between two lakes. Unless you have been reading the map carefully, these are a very pleasant surprise and their peaceful beauty make it very hard to resist a rest here. Follow the track to pass over an overflow between the two lakes, after which you will arrive once more at open farm land. Again, the track forks and you should take the right hand fork in the direction of a yellow arrow marked by the figure 10.

i The track soon runs between the wood on your right and fields on your left and after a short distance, meets a track forking left. At the same time, you will notice that the track cuts through a bank and ditch. These are ramparts to an old hill fort. The fort is particularly small and was probably a satellite fort or an overflow from the much larger fort less than a mile away at Silchester. You should ignore the track left to continue straight on.

After the fort, the fields on your left disappear and the track runs through the wood once more to soon meet a crossing track. Turn left onto the crossing track and continue through the wood, ignoring all turnings off, to eventually meet a road beside a house on your left. Cross the road and join a footpath the other side, marked by a low stump with a green arrow and horseshoe. You are now about to *i* traverse Silchester Common, which has some strict bylaws to which you must adhere. They forbid the carrying of bows, crossbows and catapults and the sports of fishing and shooting.

The footpath runs through a line of gorse which acts as a dividing line through the birch wood covering the common. As you continue, look out for a path leading off to the left, again marked by a low stump with green arrow and horseshoe, which you should take. (If you find yourself meeting a road, you will have gone too far. You can either retrace your steps or turn left along the road which will shortly lead to the same destination as the path, "The Calleva Arms"). The path runs through birch woodland, intersperced in places by willow and after a short distance, meets a crossing path. You should ignore the green arrow and horseshoe here and go over the crossing path to continue ahead.

Your route is now bordered by gorse and heather and soon leads to a playing field. Follow the right hand perimeter of the playing field and as the perimeter bends left, you should turn right instead to join a narrow path which leads through more gorse, before arriving at a lane in front of a garage, "Silchester Motor Company". Turn left and follow the lane to reach a green and "The Calleva Arms" pub, Gales. The pub is one of the most northern of the Gales brewery and apart from serving the excellent ales for which Gales are renowned, it offers good value meals and is the only place where a guide can be purchased for the old Roman town of Calleva, our next destination.

War Memorial at Silchester

To continue our route, walk

directly away from "The Calleva Arms" along the perimeter of the green, in the direction of the road sign on your right to Mortimer and Reading. As you continue, look out for a large stone memorial on your right, at which point you should cross the road and join a small grass area around the memorial which commemorates those who took part in the two World Wars. Walk behind the memorial and take a narrow path at the left hand corner of the grass area, to continue through the now familiar gorse and silver birch of Silchester Common.

On meeting a lane in front of the Calleva Museum, cross the lane and join a track, a bridleway, which runs alongside the museum. (The museum is open daily during daylight hours). Follow the track leading to Calleva and pass a number of cottages to reach and cross a stile beside a gate. You should now continue along a fenced path between fields, where after passing a stile on your left the walls of the Roman town will come into view.

It is now only a short distance before you pass through a gate to arrive at the walls to the town. Here you have a choice. You can either turn right and pass through a small wooden gate and follow the southern walls round to eventually arrive at St. Mary's church the other side (this way you will see the best of the Roman defences and you can also make a short detour into Rampier Copse (OS. 635620) to see the original ramparts of the iron age settlement, here before the Romans). Alternatively, and what I would suggest is our official route and a marked public footpath, is to continue ahead along a track which soon bends left and then right to pass through the centre of the old Roman town. Both routes have their advantages, but the choice is yours.

Keeping to the official route as mentioned, stay on the track to pass through the centre of the town. As you continue, look to the left and right and take time to consider just how big this town actually was. You can also appreciate what a seemingly high position the town was in, with views across the flat countryside from the ramparts stretching for several miles.

Calleva Atrebatum (OS. 640625 Map 175) *is unique in that at some stage it was completely abandoned, whilst most other Roman towns of a similar size grew to become major towns today, e.g. Canterbury, Colchester, St. Albans and of course, London, to name but a few. Calleva Atrebatum grew from an iron age fort, keeping its Celtic name which literally means "the town in the wood of Atrebates". It quickly became the administrative centre of Atrebates which funnily enough, covers roughly the same area of Old Berkshire, with some of north Hampshire and north west Surrey.*

The town was laid out in a grid fashion with most of the public buildings, including the Basilica and Forum, being at the centre. The walls which protected the town are a later edition, built approximately two hundred years after the town was first occupied. The reason for this is that for most of the Roman occupation England led a peaceful existence. It was only with the recalling of the garrisons by Rome to protect their frontiers from the Barbarians, that unrest started to appear in England. To protect the towns, the Romans quickly threw up defensive walls. At Calleva, the circumference of the wall is one and a half miles, in places it is three metres thick and would have had the added defence of a ditch which was approximately fourteen metres wide.

In the protection of the walls, apart from the Basilica and Forum, were several temples, a Roman church, an extensive public baths, a mansio (comparable to a coaching inn), streets with small shops as well as luxury villas and middle class housing. Outside the walls, were the equivalent of modern day suburbs. These stretched as far as half a mile from the walls in some places. All the buildings would have been well constructed, in particular the domestic housing would have offered comfort similar in standard to today. The average house had mosaic floors, central heating, glazed windows and in one case, even a private bathroom.

One of the most interesting buildings was the church, reputedly the earliest known Christian church in England. Religion during the Roman occupation was a confused affair. The Romans brought with them their classic gods and built in their honour, great temples. They could not however, convert the Pagans who continued to worship their own gods under the guidance of the Druids. Over the years, the two extreme brands of religion became entwined and Celtic-Romano temples became common. In Europe, two new religions also became popular, Mythraism from Persia and Christianity from Palestine. Mythraism became popular with the elite Roman classes, whilst Christianity was banned with followers punishable by death because of the religion's refusal to swear loyalty to the emperor. This did not stop the spread of Christianity and by the 2nd century, there were Christian sects in Britain.

It was not until 313 AD, two centuries later, that Rome finally gave in and Emperor Constantine the Great officially recognised Christianity on behalf of Rome. This was not without some concessions, one of which was that all biblical figures in future had to be shown with a light above their heads. The light was to represent the God of Light, Mithras and made acceptance of Christianity easier for the Romans. Holy figures are still represented in this way today, the light now commonly known as a halo.

The Silchester Horse

Unfortunately, apart from the walls, no traces of the Roman town are visible from the ground. Standing at what was the town centre surrounded by fields, it is hard to imagine the town as it was with its grand public buildings and streets filled with colourful robed people. There can be no greater contrast with the peaceful scene today, which begs the question, why was the town deserted? The answer remains a mystery.

As you near the far side of the town of Calleva, the track bends left in front of an old barn. You should leave it here to pass through a kissing gate ahead to your right and thereafter, bear right in the direction of a footpath sign painted on the wall of the barn. This soon leads you to a small metal gate through which you should pass to follow a fenced path around to a gate leading into the church yard of St. Mary's. (N.B. This is the point at which the alternative route rejoins our walk).

St. Mary's Church (OS. 643623 Map 175). This lovely church dates from the 12th century, seven centuries after the Romans had left Calleva. It was heavily restored by T.H. Wyatt in the 19th century, but unlike other Victorian architects Wyatt appears to have appreciated the original structure and the restoration was done in sympathy with the old style.

Inside, of particular interest is the richly carved chancel screen and an effigy thought to be of Eleanor Baynard.

Follow the path ahead to meet the church entrance and continue to exit via a wooden gate. Turn right immediately after and follow a track which runs between the old Roman wall on your right and a pretty pond on your left. The pond is part of the Roman ditch which formed part of the defences of Calleva. Pass through a parking area to meet a lane and turn left along the lane passing the entrance to the old manor house on your left, at the same time ignoring a road off to the right. Continue straight on until the lane bends left in front of a post box where you should turn right onto a signposted public footpath. Before doing this however, I suggest you take a look at the old amphitheatre which you can visit by following the lane for just a few paces, to pass through a kissing gate beside a farm gate opposite the footpath and the other side of a drive which leads off the lane on the bend.

The Amphitheatre (OS. 643626 Map 175) *enjoys a peaceful location, very different from the days when thousands would crowd here to watch a contest. The best way to experience the amphitheatre is to stand in the centre of the arena and try to imagine the scene all those centuries ago. The flint arena wall then, would have been three metres high designed to hold back spectators as well as keeping contestants in the arena. Behind the wall, wooden seating would have held up to nine thousand screaming spectators. The two recesses to the east and west may have held alters to the Greek goddess, Nemesis (Goddess of Retribution), or could simply have been rest rooms for waiting participants in the games.*

The entertainment held here could have ranged from gladiatorial combat which often resulted in death, to fights involving animals such as bull dogs or even bears. The amphitheatre was also where public executions took place.

It can certainly make you turn cold when you think what may have taken place on the spot where you are now standing.

Returning to our route, join the signposted footpath by passing through a gap in the hedge to enter a large field, where you are immediately afforded excellent views across the familiar open farm land traversed on the earlier part of this walk. Continue straight on across the centre of the field and as you progress, look out for the spire on your left of the church at Stratfield Mortimer, our starting point. If your legs are beginning to ache now and you are starting to regret buying this book, take comfort in the fact that at this point when I was checking the walk, lightening flashed and within seconds the heavens opened, leaving me soaked before I had time to don my waterproofs. Too wet to do anything, I trudged the rest of the walk without protection, returning to my car feeling more like a bath sponge than a human being and with my notes and camera in a very sorry state.

Feeling all the better I am sure for learning of my misfortune, continue to reach the far side of the field and pass between two wooden posts beside a farm gate to reach a lane. Cross the lane and follow another lane opposite signposted to Stratfield Saye, to soon pass over the Fowdry Brook and thereafter, the main railway line between Reading and Basingstoke. After the railway line, stay on the lane which follows the route of a Roman road called the Devil's Highway, for another quarter of a mile, ignoring a footpath off to the left almost opposite the driveway to a house and another on the right through the garden of the house. After this, take the next footpath on your left which goes over a stile beside a farm gate **(OS. 664626)**. Take care not to miss this as the sign is simply an arrow on the stile.

Once over the stile follow the right hand perimeter of a field to the far side and pass through a gate into the next field. Again you should follow the right hand field perimeter which soon bends right and at the corner, cross a stile beside a farm gate and continue ahead along a wide track. To your left the church spire at Stratfield Mortimer is ever prominent.

The track eventually leads out to another track coming in from the left. You should turn left and join the latter track, almost going back on yourself, which leads into a field. Follow the right hand field perimeter and when this gives way, continue along a prominent path diagonally right across the field, heading for the church spire at Stratfield Mortimer. Pass under some electricity pilons and at the far side of the field, cross a stile and carry straight on to pass under a railway bridge. At the other side of the railway line, follow a prominent path diagonally right across the centre of a field and at the far end, you will reach the footbridge crossed at the very start of our walk. Do not go over the footbridge, but turn right to retrace your steps to reach our starting point at the church at Stratfield Mortimer.

ACCOMMODATION

The Railway Inn, Stratfield Mortimer. Tel: 0734 332428
At the start of the walk, this is a recently refurbished Whitbread pub. The rooms are well furnished and comfortable and a treat to return to without the aid of a car.

Kennet House (Houseboat), Burghfield Bridge. Tel: 0734 571060
Approximately five and a half miles from the walk, accommodation is aboard a luxury houseboat, moored on the Kennet and Avon canal.

Youth Hostel, Streatley YHA, Streatley. Tel: 0491 872278
Twelve miles from the walk, the recently refurbished Streatley hostel now offers small family rooms as well as the normal dorms we all know. The hostel itself is a large Victorian house only a few paces from "The Bull Inn".

Camping & Caravanning, Wellington Country Park, Riseley. Tel: 0734 326444
Four miles from the walk, this is one of the nicest and best run camp sites I have ever had the pleasure to stay on. Pitches are set in woodland and are cleverly laid out so that you virtually have a clearing to yourself. Beside the site is a deer park and it is a real treat to laze outside your tent watching a herd pass your particular glade. Staying here also allows you free admission to the park.

THE HUNGERFORD HARE

Distance: 10¾ miles (17.25 km)
Time: Allow approximately 5 hours
Map: Ordnance Survey Landranger Map 174

THE HUNGERFORD HARE
BERKSHIRE

START	STANDEN	TEMPLETON	FINISH
HUNGERFORD	MANOR	STUD	HUNGERFORD
95M	120M	115M	95M

RIVER KENNET
START
A4
A4
TO MARLBOROUGH
TO NEWBURY
KENNET & AVON CANAL
RIVER DUN
STANDEN MANOR
HUNGERFORD
TEMPLETON
BALSDON FARM
BAGSHOT
A338
TO ANDOVER

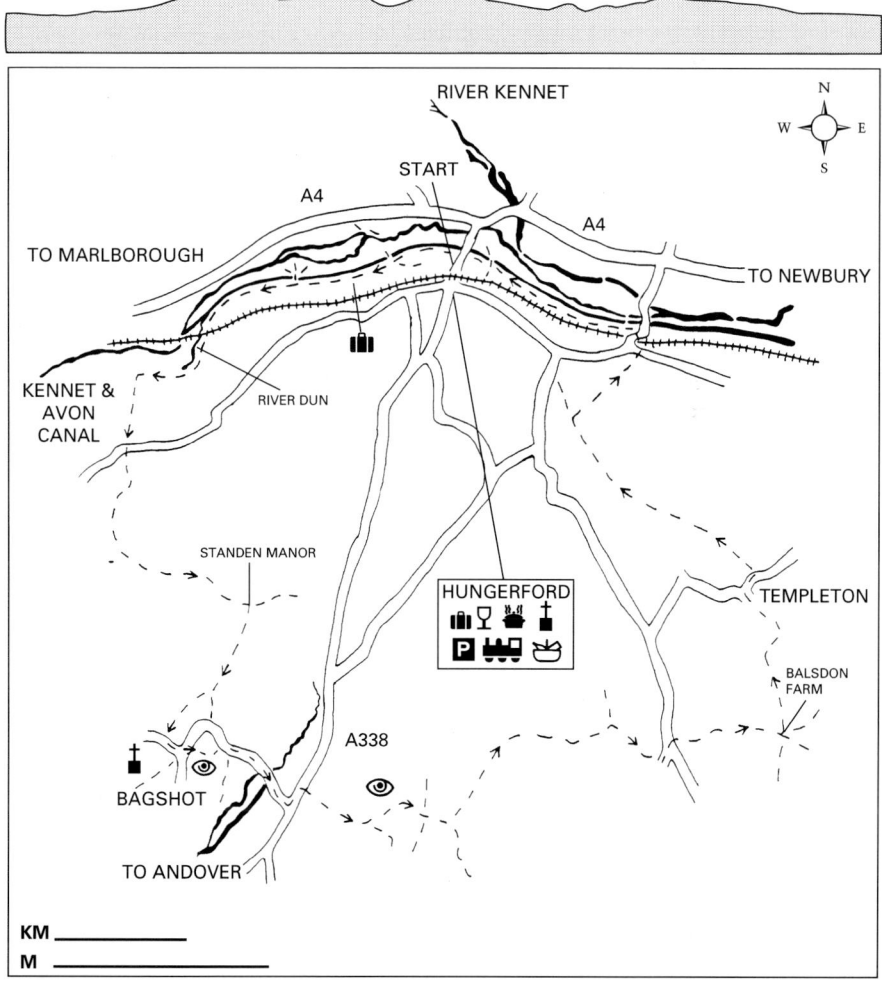

KM _____
M _____

Walk Summary

Starting from colourful Hungerford, this walk proceeds to explore some of the least known countryside in Berkshire. The scenery, particularly the woodland, is some of the best you will find in the county and with the lack of people, your chances of spotting wildlife particularly hares, is greatly increased. The going is fairly easy though as usual, some of the paths can be very muddy in wet weather. One word of warning, apart from at your starting point, there are no pubs en route. In emergencies such as this, I normally carry those small bottles of Continental beer to be enjoyed in the surroundings of my choice. I suggest you do the same, but do not forget the bottle opener!

Start - OS. 338687 Map 174

The walk starts from the northern side of the canal bridge on the High Street at Hungerford. Getting to Hungerford is relatively easy. If coming by car, Hungerford is at the junction of two main roads, the A338 Andover to Wantage road and the A4, between Marlborough and Newbury. If you are coming via the M4, exit at junction 14 and take the A338 south, signposted to Hungerford. If you arrive early, there are parking spaces alongside the High Street. These do tend to fill up very quickly, even on Sundays and when this happens, your best bet is the Pay and Display car park beside the railway station (signposted).

Hungerford also has a main line railway station which offers quite a good service. There is no obvious alternative start.

THE HUNGERFORD HARE

Hungerford is a lovely town from which to start the walk, the long High Street rising from the confluence of the rivers Dun and Kennet (rivers which have recently been recognised as being amongst the cleanest in England), is peppered with period houses and old coaching inns. Above most of the shop windows hangs the sign "Antiques" and it is hard not to be distracted by the treasure-filled windows. The town still retains a feel of affluence held over from a prosperous past, a past which I shall attempt to do justice in this book, though I recommend you buy a local guide book to fill in the gaps which I shall undoubtedly leave.

Hungerford (OS. 338687 Map 174), *surprisingly for its size, did not exist at the time of the Domesday Book. This is probably because of the extensive marsh which surrounded the confluence of the rivers Dun and Kennet, the same marsh which prompted the false story that Hingwar the Dane drowned here. The very name Hungerford is thought to describe an area of poor land around a ford. Whatever the reason, approximately one hundred years after Domesday, a prosperous town had sprung up controlled by a community of Burgesses. From this time on, Hungerford steadily grew in prosperity and helped by the busy London to Bath road, later became a market town. The people of Hungerford during this period were extremely fortunate to have a succession of good landlords. The first of these was Simon de Montfort, who granted the townsfolk the commoners right to graze their animals on land east of Hungerford, now known as Hungerford Common.*

After de Montfort came the popular John of Gaunt, who added a fishing charter to the commoners right. This charter was of great benefit to the townsfolk whose staple diet consisted mainly of fish. It became even more important after the Reformation, when eating fish was compulsory on three days of the week. To seal the charter, John of Gaunt gave the town a brass horn.

Later landlords were not so generous and in 1572, one John Lovelake attempted to seize the rights of the commoners by stealing the charters and putting a guard on the river. Turmoil followed and although Elizabeth I stepped in and ordered that the townsfolk should be restored their commoners rights, these were never redefined. Without written definition, the turmoil continued and the courts were hard pressed to cope as disputes over rights increased. In 1612 in a unique show of co-operation, the people of Hungerford eventually solved their problems by appointing a group of trustees, through whom they purchased the rights to the manor. They also acquired a significant amount of property including "The John O Gaunt Inn", which is still owned by the town today.

To this day, the trustees still manage the town and the horn presented by John of Gaunt, has become the symbol of office. It also plays a central role in an elaborate Hocktide ceremony to elect the new body of trustees. This is known locally as "Tutti Day". The proceedings start with the continuous blowing of the horn and after this, two men known as "Tuttimen" go round the town collecting the "Headpenny" or tax. To sweeten the burden of donating so much money, they drink with each householder, donate an orange and kiss the woman of the house. The whole ceremony ends at the stroke of midnight when a toast is made to John of Gaunt, after which Auld Lang Syne and God Save the Queen are sung. One final blast of the horn signals for everyone to go home.

The number of coaching inns at Hungerford is a reminder of how busy the London to Bath road was. The most famous of these is "The Bear", which was originally established in 1297. The present building is Georgian and can be found as it has been for centuries, beside the Bath road north of the canal. The inn has received many famous guests over the years, including Elizabeth I, Charles I and Samuel Pepys, though the most dramatic renting of a room must be to William III, better known as William of Orange. In 1689 whilst staying here, William accepted the throne of England after his father-in-law, James II, panicked and voluntarily gave it up. William's confirmation of the crown came with the agreement of Parliament who had little choice after James had fled abroad. However, the event set a precedent in that Parliament had the power to decide the future of the throne, something that was confirmed by the Bill of Rights in 1690. The Bill was the first step to making England a constitutional monarchy.

The many coaching inns provide a wide choice of refreshment. Running through the centre of town, there is "The Plume", Morlands, "The John O Gaunt", Morlands, "The Lamb Inn", Courage and "The Three Swans", an hotel. It would be cruel to pick any of them as they all have their own individual character. "The Bear" hotel as you would expect is of a high standard and very comfortable, but walking boots should be changed for more suitable footwear before gracing the bar! My two favourite inns are first, the "Downgate" facing Hungerford Common, which serves some of the best beer and has an amusing sign outside asking all dogs to make sure their owners have clean feet. The second, if you are seeking a true culinary experience, is "The Toad and Trout" on the Bath road. It serves, in my opinion, the best food in town and a must are the potato skins and the homemade fish cakes!

Apart from the inns, Hungerford has plenty of shops from which to buy provisions as well as a couple of cafes.

To start the walk, follow the High Street to the southern end where you will meet the bridge over the Kennet and Avon canal. Do not cross the bridge, but take a small footpath just to the left of it and join the tow path on the northern side of the canal, to head west. You are immediately met by a busy scene of brightly coloured narrow boats and their noisy neighbours, a rabble of hungry ducks awaiting the next bread laden visitor.

i **The Kennet and Avon Canal** *is in fact, three canals which were combined in the early 19th century. Before the canal, the only route from London to the West was via the Bath road, notorious for its disrepair. The turnpiking of the road in the 18th century helped, but coach and horses was still an expensive way to transport goods. By the early 18th century, there were two canals already in operation in between Wales and London. In the west the Avon Navigation, linking Bristol to Bath and in the east, the Kennet Navigation, linking Newbury to the river Thames. In 1788, Charles Dundas along with several businessmen, opened discussions on joining the two. Six years later, work was started on the fiftyfive miles from Newbury to Bath under the supervision of John Rennie.*

With the completion of a series of twentynine locks over Caen Hill, the canal was eventually opened in 1810. It was an immediate success and brought prosperity throughout the Kennet valley, at its height carrying three hundred and fortyone thousand, eight hundred and seventyeight tons of freight in a year. However, there were problems. During harsh winters the canal froze over bringing traffic to a standstill, whereas drought in summer often forced many of the larger boats to transfer their cargo to the road, at great expense. Sweet revenge for the coach companies.

The success of the railways brought an end to the canal. In 1833, Brunnel announced his proposal for a London to Bristol route. Two years later, approval was granted by the Government and by 1841, the line was complete. The towns along the route rejoiced thinking that the railway would bring even more prosperity. The joy however, was short lived for unlike the narrow boats, the trains rarely stopped and instead of trade increasing, it virtually vanished. The canal closed almost overnight and despite huge redundancies, losses kept mounting. Defeat was eventually admitted when the Kennet and Avon Canal Company sold out to the Great Western Railway (GWR). The GWR's only interest was to run the canal down and by 1955, it was unnavigable.

After strong public pressure, the Kennet and Avon Canal Trust was set up to restore the canal to its former glory. Forty years of fund raising and hard work paid off when on 8th August, 1990, Her Majesty Queen Elizabeth II officially re-opened the canal. It is now the longest linear park in the south of England, giving thousands of people pleasure every year. Details of the activities on offer and of membership to the Canal Trust can be obtained from the trust's head office: The Canal Centre, Couch Lane, Devizes, SN10 1HB. (Tel: 0380 721279).

This part of the canal is Hungerford Wharf which opened in 1798. Apart from loading and unloading goods, it was also where passenger boats were officially assessed and registered. On your immediate left, you will pass a number of pretty cottages before reaching the first lock. Here there is an information sign detailing the history of the wharf.

Follow the tow path to later pass Hungerford church on your left.

i **The Church of St. Lawrence (OS. 334687 Map 174)** *is Victorian, built in a gothic style and stands on the site of a previously Norman church. The present church was* *built in 1816 after the Norman church had all but collapsed. Its design received heavy criticism and in 1836 one of its strongest critics, Bishop Wilberforce, insisted that parishioners from Hungerford who wished to receive the sacrament had to do so at an alternative church.*

Inside, there are a few relics from the old church, the most interesting being a memorial of an old knight.

At this point, you will also meet a crossing path, the path leading off to your right going over the canal by way of a rotating bridge and the path left, to the church. Ignore both, unless you wish to visit the church and continue to follow the tow path ahead. The canal now cuts through Hungerford Marsh, a beautiful landscape of untrained grassland and extensive reed beds. The area is a site of special scientific interest. Over one hundred and twenty species of birds have been recorded here. For further details on the wildlife to be found along the canal, see "The Water Chase".

Sometime later, pass through a gate and stay on the tow path where ahead of you now is another lock, Marsh Lock. Pass a pretty thatched cottage on your left and thereafter, a low brick building, "Marshgate Cottage Hotel" (recommended accommodation). The tow path now continues through open fields, another popular place for ducks and other waterfowl.

Soon after "Marshgate Cottage Hotel", you will arrive at Marsh Lock where you should ignore a footpath over a swing bridge across the canal, to continue ahead. The tow path leaves the field, passing through a small gate beside a larger one, just before another lock. Carry straight on to reach Cobblers Lock, with its attractive lock keeper's house on the opposite bank.

On meeting the lock, take a signposted footpath left over a stile into a field. Turn immediately right and follow the right hand perimeter of the field, where shortly after on your right and just below the canal, the river Dun will come into view. At the end of the field, turn left over a stile and ascend some fairly steep steps to cross a railway line. This is the main line between London, Bristol and South Wales and great care therefore, is needed.

At the other side, go down some steps and follow a narrow footpath to cross a stile into a field. Turn right and follow the right hand field perimeter round. As you progress, look out on your right through the trees for the river Dunn and the remains of an old mill. Soon after, on meeting a track on your right, take this to enter a field on the right and follow the track along the right hand perimeter. We have now left the relative bustle of the canal and for the next few miles will explore the forgotten countryside below the North Hampshire Downs. The large open fields of this countryside are one of the few remaining strongholds of the brown hare.

The Brown Hare *was once common throughout the British Isles, but intensive farming has recently reduced their population and they now only exist in numbers in pockets, except for Scotland where they are still abundant. If you spot a hare your immediate reaction is often one of surprise, for a large hare can stand two and a half feet high and can be mistaken for a small deer. You will normally see a hare when it stands up to survey its surroundings. On the walk, it is quite possible that you may even surprise a hare feeding at the field edge. I have done this on more than one occasion, but rather than run off each time, the hare has simply looked at me as though annoyed at being disturbed and slowly ambled away. This casual behaviour probably stems from its confidence to out run any of its predators. At full pelt the* hare can run as fast as thirtyfive miles an hour.

Hares are perfectly adapted for life in the open. Unlike the rabbit the hare does not shelter in burrows, but lives all its life above ground. It breeds all year round. The young, known as leverets, are born with a full coat of fur to protect them against the elements. A litter usually numbers three with each leveret being hidden separately in a grass hollow, called a "form". In March the hares act as though they are permanently drunk leaping high in the air and participating in wild chases. At this time of year, the male tends to get a little over amorous and what appears to be a boxing match ensues, as the female fends off his unwanted advances. This eccentric behaviour has given rise to the expression, "Mad as a March hare".

Sighting this beautiful creature is always a pleasure, so keep your eyes peeled and you will not go home disappointed.

Stay on the track which later passes a small man-made pond on the right and continue to the end of the next field to meet a "T" junction in the form of a wide track. Turn left along the track which runs between hedgerows to soon meet a lane. Cross the lane and join a tarmac drive the other side, signposted as a public footpath and also "tradesman entrance". Follow the drive ahead which runs parallel to the main drive on your right to "North Standen House" and on meeting a gate to the property, bear left onto a chalk track and continue ahead around the property perimeter. The view over the property and its garden is quite magnificent, with a lovely summer house sitting quietly in the modestly formal grounds.

Continue on the chalk track and pass through a gap in the hedge ahead. Turn immediately right thereafter, thereby leaving the main track and follow the field perimeter round. At the far right hand corner of the field, stay on the track and continue ahead into the next field. As a guide, the wood on your right here is Lady's Wood, though on the Landranger Map it is marked only as the larger "Stype Wood". Follow the right hand perimeter of the field round (do not leave the field) and continue to meet a telegraph pole the other side. From here you should bear gently right across grass and after approximately thirty paces, join a narrow footpath ahead which runs through a strip of woodland **(OS. 315665)**. As a guide, you should be following the line of telegraph poles to soon meet a track in view ahead, which also follows the telegraph poles.

On joining the track, follow it ahead running west between fields heading for "Standen Manor", in view in the distance. The views ahead to your right are of Ham Hill and the North Hampshire Downs, though rest assured they are not part of our walk today. Stay on the track to reach the farm buildings of "Standen Manor" and continue ahead through the farm to meet a tarmac drive at a "T" junction. There is a small post box here on the left. Turn right along the drive and continue ahead to pass a large white house on the left. The drive soon graduates into a farm track and you should follow it between hedgerows and fields.

As the hedgerows end, continue for a few paces to meet the start of the next field and then turn right to cross it, going diagonally left across the centre **(OS. 319656)**. The field is fairly small and it is not long therefore, before you meet a stile in the far corner. Cross the stile and follow a narrow path ahead through Catmore Copse and after a short distance, make for a stile at the other side. This may take some finding, being almost hidden at the other side of a small bank. Go over the stile into a field where, as a guide, there are two thatched cottages at the far side.

Go straight across the field heading for a gate just to the right of the cottages and pass through the gate to meet a lane. Turn left along the lane which takes you through the pretty hamlet of Bagshot. You will be glad to know that at 149m, Bagshot is the highest point on our walk. Continue to meet a "T" junction beside a small brick chapel on your right. To meet the "T" junction, the lane forks around a triangular green. You should take the left hand fork and continue ahead to cross a lane and pass through a farm gate the other side into a field. Carry straight on along a grass track across the centre of the field, where to your right there are more good views of Ham Hill. At the far side, the track you are following begins to descend and at the same time, bends gently left to enter Westcott Copse.

After a short distance, you will arrive at a farmyard, part of "Upper Slope End Farm". Walk straight through the farmyard and pass through a metal gate to meet a lane. Turn right along the lane and follow it downhill, passing "Old Mill House" on your right, the name denoting its true function in days of old. Continue over two bridges across two streams which feed the mill and stay on the lane to meet the main road, the A338.

Turn left along the A338 and pass "The Courtyard" on your left. After approximately fifty metres, look out for a footpath sign at the other side of the road. Cross the road, pass through a metal gate and join the signposted footpath mentioned. After a short distance, you will meet a number of gates. You should carry straight on here along a fenced grass track which soon enters Kiln Copse. Take care, this can be somewhat overgrown in summer and protective clothing may be helpful in warding off those hidden nettles! The path leads gently uphill and follows a stream on the right. As the field on your left ends, you should continue straight on through Kiln Copse along the path which at this point, also shares its route with the stream and can therefore be extremely muddy. At the far side of the copse, exit via a wooden gate and continue straight on across a field to meet a tarmac drive in front of a pond.

Turn right along the drive and after approximately twenty metres, turn left in the direction of a public footpath sign. You will now walk between a line of mature trees on the left and newly planted ones on the right. After the avenue of trees ends, continue straight on bearing gently right and head for the corner of the field. The views left now are quite superb. When I last walked this way I saw no less than four hares in the field, all of whom knew their speed and agility could easily whisk them away from my natural inquisitiveness and therefore, appeared quite non-plussed by my presence.

Go over a stile at the corner of the field and thereafter, over a small stream and continue to follow a fairly prominent but narrow winding path through a wood. As before, this is one of the less well known paths and therefore, can be somewhat overgrown in summer. Its benefit however, is that it is still very untouched and preserves its naturual beauty, lost in so many of our managed woods.

After a short distance, you will arrive at a footpath sign in front of a small stream. Turn right here after crossing the stream, onto a more prominent path and follow the stream gently uphill. This part of the wood is particularly beautiful. As you progress, you may be surprised to see a small pond on your right with resident ducks, albeit not as welcoming as most, not used to having many visitors.

i

Continue for a few paces beyond the pond to meet a stile at the end of the wood. Go over the stile which is quite a steep stepped stile and continue straight on initially following the field perimeter. My fortune in enjoying the local wildlife when writing this walk, stayed with me. For it was at this point, whilst studying the map, that I spotted an Ermine bounding along the field perimeter towards me. An Ermine for the unitiated, is a stoat with a coat that has turned white for winter camouflage. It is rare to see an Ermine this far south, as the colour change normally only happens to stoats in the north of England and Scotland where there are heavy snows. Suddenly, the Ermine realised my presence and after standing on its hind legs to confirm it, darted off in a panic.

Going back to our walk, as the field perimeter bends away to your right, you should continue straight ahead across the centre of the field. Look out for a footpath sign ahead which indicates a junction of paths and on reaching this, take the left hand path across the centre of the field, where as a guide, you should now have woodland on your right, Anvilles Copse and further away on your left, the woods we have just left.

The way across the field is very undefined. Therefore, as you near the other side, head for a gate and stile marked by a small yellow footpath sign. Go over the stile and carry straight on along a prominent path, again through woodland, to shortly run gently downhill. The woodland here is deciduous and as ever, very picturesque and home to a mass of wildlife.

On nearing the end of the wood, the path passes over a stream and runs through a thick line of conifers to reach a farm track. Turn right along the track to immediately pass through a farm gate and carry straight on along the track which crosses the centre of a field. As a guide, "Anvilles Farm" can be seen ahead to your left.

At the far side of the field, cross a stile and take a signposted footpath diagonally right heading for a gate and another footpath sign. Pass through the gate and go straight on in the direction of the footpath sign, just to the left of a track which runs across the centre of the field, to reach a stile at the far side. The stile is in fact in the far left hand corner of the field. Go over the stile and turn left to follow the left hand perimeter of the next field (you should ignore the footpath sign here indicating that you should go straight across the field). On reaching the corner, go over a stile and carry straight on across another field, with a scattering of oak and silver birch trees.

At the end of the field, cross a stile and continue ahead through a small paddock with a tennis court on the right and some outbuildings on the left. You will soon arrive at a drive way. Turn right along the drive and follow it to pass to the left of a large house, "Totterdown House". The drive soon meets the main tarmac drive to "Totterdown House" onto which you should turn left. You will now be walking away from the house and should continue going gently downhill to cross over a small stream. Thereafter, follow the drive uphill to meet a lane.

Turn left along the lane, ignoring a footpath the other side and at a "T" junction where the lane forks, take the left hand fork and cross the lane ahead to join a signposted bridleway the other side. The bridleway runs through woodland and initially runs adjacent to a garden on your right. Thereafter, it goes downhill and in wet weather can be very muddy. At the other side of the wood go through a wooden gate and cross a field ahead in the direction of the bridleway sign.

At the far side of the field, pass through another wooden gate and cross a small stream to continue ahead through more woodland, still following a prominent bridleway. The bridleway now runs slowly uphill and as you progress passes through an area of scotch pines. Soon after, you should follow the bridleway signs to continue ahead across a field, heading to the right of a farmhouse ahead. To your right on a clear day, are more excellent views of the North Hampshire Downs, including Walbury Hill and just visible, Combe Gibbet.

At the far side of the field do not join the drive ahead, but turn left just before it and follow the right hand field perimeter, marked as a public footpath. Pass the farmhouse on your right, "Balsdon Farm", a manor house recorded in the Domesday Book. Behind the farm is an old moat, the only existing remains of the old fortified manor which once stood here. At the corner of the field, go straight on passing through a gap in the hedge and then over a small stile into another field. Go straight across the centre of the field following a well trodden path and at the other side on meeting a wood, turn right to follow the field perimeter. After a short distance, you will meet a stile beside a metal gate. Go over the stile and turn left to follow a track downhill through the wood.

You should ignore any turnings off to the left or right and continue along the track which soon bends left to run parallel with a field on your left. Pass through a gate ahead and thereafter, bear right to reach a tarmac drive in front of an Estate Office for "Templeton Stud". The name Templeton comes from the old manor which belonged to the Knights Templar. Turn left and follow a tarmac drive to pass through a white gate onto a lane. Turn right along the lane and after approximately one hundred metres, take a signposted footpath on your left. This leads across the centre of a field along a prominent path, where at the far side you should cross over a small stream and then turn right to follow the perimeter of the next field round (do not leave the field). Shortly after, you will meet a hedged grass track which you should take.

The track runs parallel to some woodland on your right and thereafter continues along the right hand perimeter of a field. Please note, as a the woodland ends, you should ignore a track leading off to the right. As you progress, there are more good views left over the North Hampshire Downs. The field is a long one and on eventually reaching the far side, you should go straight over a crossing track and continue ahead along the right hand perimeter of the next field. Ahead to your left, the first signs of Hungerford are now visible, including the school, a long brick building with a small tower.

Like the previous field, this field is also a long one. On nearing the end, look out for a beech tree on the right with a vast number of carvings on its trunk. Thereafter, you should cross a stile ahead to arrive at Hungerford Common. Turn right here and follow the perimeter of the common keeping the woodland on your right. The route takes you gently downhill and soon crosses a drive way to a picturesque gate house on your right. Sometime after, still with the woodland on your right, you will arrive at a lane beside a small parking area.

Turn left along the lane and after approximately twenty metres, turn right onto a smaller lane, signposted to Lower Denford. You will immediately cross the main London to Bristol railway line and should follow the road round to pass in front of a large pill box. It is only a short distance before we rejoin the Kennet and Avon canal. Do not cross a bridge over the canal, but turn left just before it onto the tow path in the direction of the signs for Hungerford. You will immediately pass Dun Mill Lock which in summer is often busy with day trippers.

Just after the lock, you will pass "Dun Mill" on the opposite bank, which sits conveniently at the confluence of the rivers Dun and Kennet. Go over a stile and continue along the tow path for a distance of three quarters of a mile, to reach Hungerford. As you enter Hungerford you will pass through a white gate in front of a pretty bridge across the canal. Ignore the bridge and continue ahead along the tow path to reach a second bridge. Leave the tow path here and turn left to arrive at the main High Street at Hungerford, our starting point. Your only problem now, is which coaching inn to choose to celebrate your completion of the walk!

ACCOMMODATION

The Bear Hotel, Hungerford. Tel: 0488 682512
On the walk, this is the place to stay if you want to treat yourself. There are rooms in the hotel itself or in the courtyard which overlooks the river Dun. All rooms are of a high standard.

Marshgate Cottage Hotel, Hungerford. Tel: 0488 682307
On the walk, this is a lovely place to stay and can only enhance your enjoyment of the area. Accommodation is in a tasteful extension to a beautiful thatched cottage. All the rooms overlook the canal and across to Freemans Marsh.

Youth Hostel, The Court Hill Ridgeway Centre YHA. Tel: 02357 60253
Nine miles from the walk, this is a purpose built hostel from the reconstruction of four barns. The hostel is in a beautiful position with views over the Vale of the White Horse. The grounds include a wood where you can camp and has a barbecue area.

Camping and Caravanning, Oakley Farm Caravan Park, Washwater. Tel: 0635 36581
Ten miles from the walk, this is an attractive site close to the outskirts of Newbury.

N.B. If you are a Camping and Caravan Club member, you can stay at Holt Lodge Farm, near Kintbury. Tel: 04884 244. For membership details, tel: 0203 694995.

TEACHER'S TEST

Distance: 11¾ miles (19 km)
Time: Allow approximately 6 hours
Map: Ordnance Survey Landranger Map 174 and 175

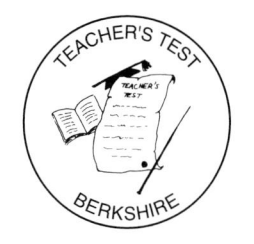

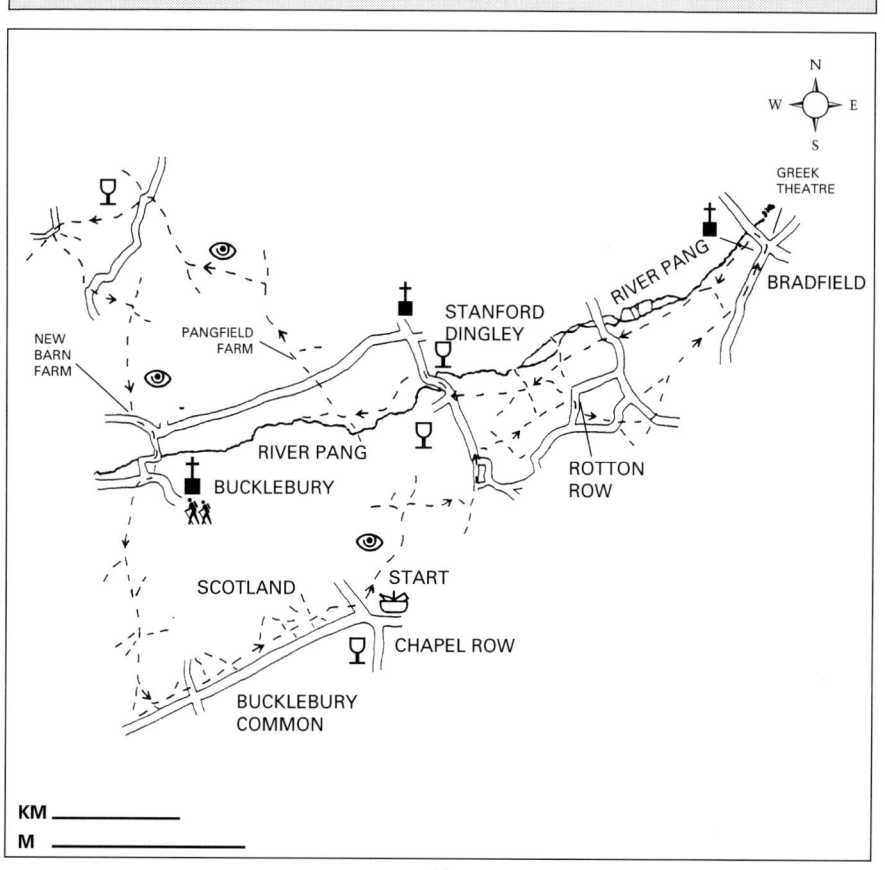

| START
CHAPEL ROW
114M | BRADFIELD
60M | BUCKLEBURY
65M | FINISH
CHAPEL ROW
114M |

Walk Summary

The Teacher's Test explores the lovely Pang valley, a part of Berkshire overlooked by developers and tourists, thereby retaining the peaceful beauty which allows for good walking. The walk takes you through a wide variety of landscapes which change with a frequency that will constantly hold your interest. The going is fairly easy with any ascents being low and gradual, the only real difficulty being mud. In wet weather, especially near the bottom of the valley along the banks of the river Pang, the going can get particularly bad, so make sure you wear those boots. Finally, I suggest you pace yourself carefully. The second half of the walk is harder than the first, with a long climb near the end. This can be quite taxing if you have raced around the earlier part of the walk.

Start - OS. 571697 Map 174

The walk starts in front of "The Blade Bone Inn" at Chapel Row. To get there, if coming from the east, make for junction 12 on the M4 and from there take the A4 to Newbury. At the first roundabout, turn right onto the A340 and follow this for a short distance to take the first turning left, signposted to Bradfield, Ashampstead, Yattendon and Compton. Follow this for approximately one and a quarter miles to then take another turning left, signposted to Southend and Bucklebury. Stay on this road until after approximately two and a quarter miles, you reach Chapel Row and "The Blade Bone Inn". If coming from the north and north east, make for Pangbourne and from there take the A340 south. Shortly after passing under the M4, take a turning right, signposted to Bradfield. Stay on the road until you reach a "T" junction beside a war memorial and here turn right and continue to reach Chapel Row. If coming from the west, take the A4 from Newbury and at Thatcham, take a turning left in front of an old chapel, signposted to Upper Bucklebury. Stay on the road to eventually reach Chapel Row, a distance of approximately four miles.

The nearest train station is Midgham Station. At weekends trains stop here roughly every two hours. The only real alternative start is Bucklebury village (OS. 552709 Map 174). Starting here means you avoid the long climb at the end.

TEACHER'S TEST

Standing beneath the unusual sign of "The Blade Bone Inn", it is probably better to satisfy our curiosity now rather than at the end of the walk.

Chapel Row (OS. 571697 Map 174) *is less well known than its two main landmarks, an avenue of oak trees and the blade bone which gave the pub its name. Indeed, if you ask anyone in Berkshire where "The Blade Bone Inn" is, they will probably tell you Bucklebury. Such is the anonymity of this scattered village. The blade bone itself, as local legend would have you believe, is from a mammoth which terrorised the local inhabitants until as one, they trapped and killed it, burying the beast on the banks of the river. Unfortunately, (for the story is a good one), the bone is actually* from a whale and was found at the beginning of the 17th century in the Kennet valley. The sign above your head is meant to be the actual bone encased in copper. Why it should be hanging from this particular inn is a mystery, though it has been suggested that it was once used to signify that the inn sold whale oil, commonly used during the 19th century as a fuel for lamps.

The huge avenue of oaks lining the road to Bradfield was planted to commemorate the visit of Elizabeth I to Bucklebury in 1568. The road then, it is believed, was the drive to "Bucklebury House", more of which we will learn later. The avenue was later added to in celebration of victory at the Battle of Trafalgar. More recently, the tradition was upheld when in 1972 new trees were planted to welcome Queen Elizabeth II. The most recent planting was by Princess Anne. On this occasion, it was a birthday present to Queen Elizabeth the Queen Mother on her eightieth birthday. With such enthusiasm for green fingered tradition, the avenue of oaks will probably welcome people to Chapel Row for centuries to come.

The village of Chapel Row itself is a scattering of houses with no apparent planned centre. This is probably because Chapel Row started as a settlement for travellers, who then made themselves permanent homes on the surrounding common. "The Blade Bone Inn" is a Whitbread pub and as well as serving bar meals, has an a la carte restaurant.

To start our walk, take the lane opposite the pub signposted to Bucklebury Village and Stanford Dingley. After approximately fifty metres, turn right onto a public bridleway, also signposted to "Apple Trees" and "Orchard View". This is beside a beautiful thatched cottage, "The Old Bakehouse".

The bridleway leads initially between houses and thereafter between fields, with just the occasional house en route. As you progress, a valley opens out to your right and you will soon pass two properties on your right, which overlook and are adjacent to orchards, hence the names "Apple Trees" and "Orchard View". After the properties, the scenery becomes more rural and on your left a gate allows an early view of the wide sweep of the Pang valley.

Stay on the track, which can be very muddy in wet weather, descending gradually and follow it as it bends gently left. The track drops into the Pang valley where you should ignore a track leading off to the left, signposted as a bridleway, and continue to meet and pass through a metal gate. Thereafter, turn right in the direction of a yellow footpath arrow and follow the right hand perimeter of a field, again with views left over the Pang valley. At the far side of the field, cross over a stile into Kings Copse and follow a path ahead. Just after, you will cross over a small stream where you should ignore a path off to the left, to continue straight on now going uphill.

Approximately half way up the hill the path divides into three. You should take the left hand path signposted "footpath only". This soon bends left where you should ignore another path off to the right, to continue your route along the footpath which then bends right to climb the side of Clay Hill. Immediately after, ignore two paths off to the left.

You will soon meet a stile beside a metal gate which you should cross to follow the path ahead. Shortly after, you will meet a drive to a large house. Follow the drive ahead and stay on it as it bends left away from the house. If you look carefully as you walk, there is a pond on the left. Ignore all turnings off to the left and right and follow the drive to meet a "T" junction in front of a white cottage, aptly named "White Cottage". You should leave the drive at this point and join a path ahead, signposted as a bridleway, which runs to the right of "White Cottage" and thereafter, along the perimeter of two properties before descending the northern slope of Clay Hill.

After a short distance, the bridleway leads out onto a lane beside a red brick house on your left. Continue straight on along the lane and after approximately thirty metres, turn right onto a signposted bridleway, just in front of the first house on your right. The house has a dovecot in its garden and the doves offer a pleasant distraction as you walk.

The bridleway initially runs parallel with the house on your left and thereafter, winds through a strip of woodland. This soon gives way on your left to afford yet more views over the Pang valley. The going here can be extremely muddy in wet weather and if you have forgotten your walking boots, you are about to regret it! Apart from the mud, be wary of the wood on your right, for it is said that the ghost of a veiled woman walks under the shelter of the trees. Sometime on, ignore a footpath and stile off to the left and thereafter, a path off to the right to carry straight on.

When the path forks, you should take the left hand fork still following the left hand perimeter of the wood. The path soon arrives at an open field, where you should continue ahead along the right hand perimeter. The view left now is over almost the entire Pang valley with the houses behind to your left, making up the village of Stanford Dingley. The farm directly below is "Kimberhead Farm". Follow the field perimeter ignoring all turnings off and at the far side, follow the path as it again skirts the perimeter of the wood.

The path eventually leads you to a gravel drive and a small cluster of houses known as Rotten Row. You should ignore a footpath off to the left here and continue straight on along the drive to reach a lane beside a small green. Turn right uphill along the lane and at the top of the hill, turn left onto a signposted footpath. You may however, want to pause here not just to regain your breath, but to look back over the hamlet of Rotten Row which to me from here, has the appearance of a Cornish fishing village rather than a Berkshire hamlet.

Follow the footpath, ignore a drive way left and continue to pass through some wooden rails. Thereafter, take a narrow footpath ahead running between banks, which support a line of holly trees that meet overhead, creating a damp, green tunnel. After a short distance, the path passes under a small brick bridge, a bridge perfect for a troll if ever there was one, and continues in a straight line to eventually meet a lane beside a house on your right, "Cherry Orchard". Go straight across the lane and go over a stile to join a signposted public footpath the other side. Do not make the mistake of taking the signposted public bridleway.

Crossing the stile takes you into a field, where you should turn left to shortly meet and cross another stile into the next field. Bear gently right across the field and

"A bridge perfect for a troll"

cross a third stile at the far side to enter another field. Again, you should bear gently right across the field, following a prominent path. At the far corner of the field, you will arrive at a lane. Cross the lane and join a track the other side which is signposted as a footpath. This runs in a straight line and acts as a natural divide between fields.

At the far side of the fields, pass through a wide gap in a hedge and continue ahead, still following the grass track between fields. As a guide, there is a picturesque, large and half tiled property ahead to your left, "Horse Leas". On reaching the end of the fields, pass through a kissing gate and carry straight on across the next field and on meeting the field perimeter, pass through another kissing gate to arrive at a tarmac drive to "Horse Leas".

Cross the drive, pass through a gap in a well manicured yew hedge and then go through a kissing gate into a long field. Go straight across the field where on your left is a long tree lined drive way, another entrance to "Horse Leas". The footpath passes a lonely scotch pine at the centre of the field and then bears gently left to head for the far corner, beside a gatehouse to "Rectory Lodge", part of Bradfield College.

Pass through some wooden railings onto a driveway and turn right to almost immediately meet a road. Turn left and follow the road into Bradfield, taking care of the traffic as you do so. It is only a short distance before a pavement begins on the left. Just after, you will be greeted by some very austere buildings belonging to Bradfield College, which has its home in the village of Bradfield.

Bradfield (OS. 605726 Map 175) *has a different air about it than the other villages of the Pang valley. This is probably because of its famous college which dominates the centre of the village and village life. Again, unlike the other villages of the Pang valley, Bradfield cannot be called "sleepy". Students and teachers alike walk the streets in purposeful fashion (yes, even the students!), often in their robes of learning, bringing a certain dignity to the village. On the playing fields to your left, you will be unlucky not to see the gentlemens' games of cricket (in summer) or rugby (in winter), being played with great gusto - no place for losers here.*

Before the college, Bradfield was like any other village in the valley, a community taking its living from the land and the river. The first evidence of any settlement is Roman. A Roman terracota lamp and some foundations were discovered beside the old workhouse in Union Road. The village appears to have continued untroubled until the Civil War, when in 1644 armies from both sides were encamped around the village, using Bucklebury Common for cover. The manoeuvres were part of the second Battle of Newbury, which like so many other battles decided nothing, but created a lot of misery.

The start of the college which was to change the face of the village, came in 1850 when one Thomas Stevens inherited the manor and "Bradfield Place". Stevens was a Rector and his dedication to his faith governed that his attention was given to the 14th century village church which he commissioned the architect, Gilbert Scott, to rebuild. The enlarged church lacked a choir, the local population being far too small to support one. To solve the problem, Stevens started a school at "Bradfield Place". The school served two purposes, it provided young voices for the choir and at the same time, it was a good Christian deed to provide young people who would normally have missed out, with an education.

Apart from the school, later the college, Stevens set about improving village life in other ways. He introduced the use of one of the first milking machines and opened a mineral water plant at St. Andrews Well. He also set up the village workhouse, which later became a hospital for the mentally handicapped, but has recently been closed. The school grew rapidly as Stevens' other ventures drained his financial resources. Eventually, he was declared bankrupt and the school was taken over by a group of trustees, who employed Doctor Herbert Gray as headmaster. Dr. Gray turned Bradfield College into one of the best schools in the country, for which people were prepared to pay great sums to secure entry for their offspring.

Dr. Gray was also responsible for building the famous copy of an open air Greek theatre in the college grounds. The theatre was cleverly constructed from an old chalk pit, the stage itself built in the form of a Greek temple as laid down by the original Greek playwrites. Today, the theatre is renowned and performances are always guaranteed a full audience.

On meeting a crossroads turn left in the direction of the sign to Ashampstead, Yattendon and Compton and go downhill. As you continue, notice a white house on the left with an unusual door knocker in the shape of a snake. Thereafter, look out for a driveway on your left beside the Pang river, signposted as a byway and to the parish church which you should now follow. This is the old centre of the village and without a doubt, the most picturesque.

The byway runs alongside the river Pang with two small private bridges accessing some delightful cottages on the opposite bank. Pass to the left of the old mill and continue round passing to the right of the parish church. The church is normally locked, but if you are lucky and the door is open, a visit is a must. The modernisation by Gilbert Scott, unlike so many other Victorian alterations, is quite stylish. After the church, pass "Cray Cottage" and go through some iron railings to continue along a path on the left hand bank of the river. Shortly after, ignore a track off to your left and also a bridge over the river on your right. Your surroundings now are delightful. To your left, the rich green playing fields of Bradfield College rise to meet an elegant pavillion and the school church. On your right, the river Pang flows with a joyous rythm in accompaniment with the melody of bird song from meadows the other side.

i

Marsh Marigolds

The scene is too good to pass quickly by.

We now leave the delights of Bradfield by passing through a kissing gate to follow the river through the more familiar open fields of the valley.

Marsh Marigolds. *In spring, the banks of the river Pang are dotted with great clumps of marsh marigolds. These colourful plants, rather like large buttercups, are one of the first to wake after the slumber of winter and can be a welcome sight in the late snows of March. It is believed that Shakespeare was rejoicing the marsh marigold when writing "Cymbeline" and penned the line, "winking Mary-*

buds begin to open their golden eyes". Farmers once believed that marsh marigolds helped to prevent their cattle falling sick, which they blamed on the trickery of fairies and witches. To protect their cattle year round, the farmers would on May Day, adorn their cattle sheds with the flower. This apparently was enough to defeat any ideas that a fairy or witch might have of doing mischief amongst the herd. Whether or not it worked, the farms at this time must have been a colourful sight.

Sometime on, cross over a stile and continue ahead along the right hand perimeter of a field, with the river Pang now concealed behind hedges on your right. At the far side of the field, pass through some wooden rails and continue along the right hand perimeter of the next field. The river is no longer visible on your right. Your way is now bordered by woodland.

Continue to follow the right hand field perimeter until you eventually meet a lane. Turn right along the lane and immediately after the entrance to "Bradfield Hall", turn left and pass through a kissing gate to follow a signposted public footpath along the left hand perimeter of a field. This is another lush green field and at the far side, a line of trees marks the course of the river Pang. As you progress, you will gain good views left through gaps in the hedgerow of the very grand "Bradfield Hall" and its ornate clock tower.

At the far side of the field, pass through a kissing gate and continue straight on along a well defined path following the perimeter of a wood. To your right here is a small but pretty oxbow pond. After a short distance, pass through another kissing gate beside a farm gate and carry straight on along a track, ignoring a smaller gate initially off to your right. A few paces on, you should also ignore a signposted bridleway left. The houses in the distance on your left, belong to Rotten Row, through which we passed earlier and beyond it, the edge of the woodland followed during the earlier stages of our walk.

At the end of the field, ignore a stile on your left and continue ahead through a gap in the hedge to follow the right hand perimeter of the next field. Shortly after entering the field, you should ignore a small crossing path to continue ahead, still following the right hand field perimeter. To your right now, there is an attractive pond nestling under some scotch pines.

Go over a stile at the far side of the field and as before, carry straight on along the right hand perimeter of the next field. Ahead of you now, the houses of Stanford Dingley come into view. Approximately half way across the field, you will meet a stile beside a metal gate ahead. Go over the stile and continue ahead along a track, heading for Stanford Dingley, our next destination. After a short distance, you will arrive at three farm gates and in between them, a smaller wooden gate. Pass through the latter, signposted as a footpath, and continue ahead along the left hand perimeter of a field. You will soon meet a stile which you should cross to carry straight on along a track.

As you approach the first buildings of Stanford Dingley, you will meet a farm gate and stile. Go over the stile and continue ahead to meet a lane. Turn right along the lane in the direction of the sign to Burnt Hill and Yattendon. The lane passes an old barn on your right and then bends left to go over the river Pang, where on your left there is a beautiful old mill house complete with mill pond. Soon after, you will arrive at the village green and the first sign of real refreshments in the form of "The Bull", a 15th century inn, now a Bass pub, a grand welcome to Stanford Dingley.

Stanford Dingley (OS. 575715 Map 174) is the sort of village that you instantly want to put on canvas to preserve the memory in your own home for it does not matter which way you turn, there is another corner put here for the artist. At the heart of Stanford Dingley is the old mill which has been here at least since Norman times and was probably the founder of the village. Any milling stopped long ago, but the mill lives on, converted into a perfect home. There are many other houses of equal beauty and far too many to relate here. My suggestion is that you discover them for yourself.

The name Stanford Dingley like so many other village names in Berkshire, is derived from the original Lord of the Manor, in this case, William de Stanford. The second half, Dingley, was added two hundred years later after another important resident, Richard Dyneley, whose father was bodyguard to Henry VI. This could not have been an enviable position, as Henry VI was one of the least popular Kings of our land and during his reign many attempts were made on his life. One wonders what the local residents attitude was to Richard Dyneley, I doubt if he was popular with such close associations to Henry VI. Even so, the man made impression enough for his name to be remembered centuries later as part of the village.

Remembered in the church which lies at the northern end of the village, is another important resident of Stanford Dingley, Thomas Teasdale, a tailor who with the fortune he made, went on to found Pembroke College, Oxford. Another resident, Dr. Richard Valpy, became headmaster in 1781 of the famous Reading School. The church itself is a tiny affair, hiding behind a curtain of majestic Spanish chestnut trees. The original building was Saxon and there are a few traces of the original masonry in the wall at the west side of the nave. The present church dates, in the main, from the 13th century and inside has some interesting features. To gain entry, you will currently have to apply for the key from "Kents Bungalow" opposite. The door through which you pass to enter the church, is probably the original and serves as well today as it did when it was built. There are some interesting medieval tiles on the church wall and some well preserved brasses, one of Margaret Dyneley and another of John Lydford, who like Teasdale, became wealthy through selling cloth made at Stanford Dingley. There are some paintings too, probably from the 13th century, one you can just make out features bodies rising from their coffins on Judgement Day.

There are two other buildings which deserve a mention and you will be pleased to know, they are the village hostelries. One I have already mentioned is "The Bull" inn, conveniently sited for some well deserved refreshment. Perhaps the most startling feature of this pub is its sign. This as you would expect depicts a bull; but unlike conventional signs, this one has the bull's head on one side and its rear in full glory on the other. Jackie was going to sketch it for inclusion in this book, but later thought better of it - we will leave you to have the pleasure of discovering it for yourself!

The second is "The Old Boot Inn", a free house. This is a pretty pub at the southern end of the village offering a wide selection of fine ales, good bar meals and has an a la carte restaurant.

Continue walking through the village passing its enviable collection of picture postcard houses and cottages, until you arrive at the church. Leave the lane here and turn left over a stile into a field and continue along the right hand perimeter. This is signposted as a public footpath and as a guide is the first and not the second footpath on the left, and is just before "Kents Bungalow".

As the garden perimeter on your right ends, continue straight on across the field along a fairly prominent path. At one point you will meet the right hand field perimeter and shortly after, leave it as the path bends gently left across the field to meet a gate, visible at the far side. The field can be extremely muddy and marshy in wet weather - real walking boot or wellie terrain! As you near the gate, you will see the river Pang on the left. Pass through the gate taking note of the distinctive sign by a budding local comic and continue ahead along a prominent path through some attractive woodland. In spring, the woodland floor here is a carpet of bluebells.

After a short distance, pass over a small stream and thereafter, over a stile into a field. Continue ahead across the field bearing gently right. On meeting a bridleway at the end of the field, turn right and follow a track across another field heading for a farm gate. To your right is a newly built pond, an attempt to encourage and develop the wildlife in the area.

At the farm gate mentioned, go over a stile beside it and continue along a farm track ahead. Do not make the mistake of taking a signposted footpath left. As you progress along the track, take time to stop and look back at the view and the earlier stages of our walk, particularly the Pang valley. On reaching a lane, cross this and continue along a drive opposite to "Pangfield Farm", also signposted as a public bridleway. Follow the drive to the farmhouse and pass it continuing through the farm yard and follow the signposted bridleway through the farm buildings to thereafter, go gently uphill between banks.

You will now follow the bridleway for some distance, gently up the north side of the Pang valley. This initially runs between fields and later, along the perimeter of a wood on your left. Again, in spring you will enjoy the vibrant colours of bluebells and daffodils here. Eventually, you will meet a prominent path on your left which leads uphill through the wood. You should join this and continue your climb in a straight line through the wood, where at the top you will arrive at a newly planted area of woodland on your right, affording excellent views beyond. The large building on the hill at the other side of the valley is "Yattendon Court".

Stay on the bridleway and ignore all turnings off until you reach a crossing track and footpath sign (**OS. 555726 Map 174).** Turn right here onto the signposted public footpath which leads gently downhill through deciduous woodland and soon after, uphill through fir trees, all this being part of High Copse. You should ignore all turnings off to the left or right. As the fir trees end, you will meet a crossing track which you should ignore to continue ahead along a path the other side, signposted as a public footpath. This leads downhill through more attractive deciduous woodland, intersperced by laurels.

After a short distance, go over a stile into a field where ahead of you now is the welcome sight of "The Pot Kiln" pub, our next destination. Carry straight on along the right hand perimeter of the field, still going downhill and approximately half way across, go over a small stream and continue ahead to reach a stile beside a farm gate. Go over the stile to meet a lane and turn left along the lane for approximately twenty metres to arrive at "The Pot Kiln", a free house with a pretty beer garden.

"The Pot Kiln", named after a pottery that once existed here, is one of those rare pubs which remains untouched by modern interior designers. Inside, there are three bars, the first being little more than a porch where more than three people become a crowd. The decor is simple and wood abounds, preserving the memories of happy drinkers from years past. Outside, there is a pretty walled garden which juts out into a field, the latter often home to a number of inquisitive sheep. To refresh you, the pub serves some basic bar meals as well as an excellent choice of real ales.

To continue, albeit reluctantly, go over a stile in front of the pub into a field and continue following the pub garden perimeter. As the garden ends, continue straight on across the centre of the field which as you progress, narrows to act as a dividing line between woodland. Thereafter, it opens out again where you should continue going straight on, now following the left hand perimeter of the field. Half way across, you will meet a footpath sign at what was the original perimeter, a reassuring sign that you are on the right route.

On nearing the end of the field just before a charming Victorian house, look out for a small kissing gate on your left through which you should pass to follow a fenced path. As the path ends, pass through another kissing gate onto a lane. Continue straight ahead along the lane and ignore a signposted public bridleway on your left. You will now pass a number of houses which make up the hamlet of Frilsham. After approximately fifty metres, you will meet a signposted footpath on your left which you should join by passing through a kissing gate. If however, you continue along the lane for a further fifty metres, you will enjoy superb views across Frilsham and over the upper reaches of the Pang valley. You will however, need to retrace your steps to rejoin our walk.

After passing through the kissing gate, ignore two footpaths signposted left and right respectively and continue ahead along a narrow path which runs downhill through Hawkridge Wood. Stay on the path which later bends gently right to head south. If in doubt here, you should make for a field visible ahead. Just before a bank and the field mentioned, follow the path as it bends left to run parallel to the bank and field, now on your right. Stay on the path which continues downhill and go over a small stream and continue, following a line of mature beech trees. As the latter ends, you must ignore a path left to maintain your route ahead along a now very narrow path. This soon bends sharp right to arrive at a stile which you should cross into a field.

Go straight across the field, heading to the left of "Hawkridge Farm" visible ahead. As you progress, take care not to twist an ankle or fall into one of the many rabbit holes which are dotted like traps all over the field. At the far corner of the field, cross a stile to meet a lane onto which you should turn right. After approximately thirty paces leave the lane and join a signposted public footpath on your left, taking time before you do so to admire the setting enjoyed by "Hawkridge Farm", with its own pond and island, complete with weeping willow and resident geese.

The path runs through undergrowth for a short distance and can be a little overgrown in summer - protective leggings are a necessity! Cross over a stile into a field where the views right are over the now familiar Pang valley. Once in the field, bear left and head to the left of a wooded hollow where you should cross another stile into the next field. Continue straight on along the left hand field perimeter until you meet a stile on your left. Do not cross this, but turn right instead for approximately fifteen paces and cross another stile into a field. You should follow the right hand perimeter of the field until this gives way and then continue straight on along a track which now runs between fields. When I last walked this way, the fields here were full of very inquisitive pigs, which provided an entertaining interlude - they were however (and luckily) fenced off!

After approximately half a mile, you will near the farm buildings of "New Barn Farm", where the track bends right to enter the farm yard. Do not follow it, but leave it here and continue ahead to meet a stile. Cross this into a field and go straight across the field to meet and cross another stile and arrive at a lane. Turn left along the lane, now heading for Bucklebury, whose church tower is just visible on the right. The lane passes a small copse on your left, home to several families of noisy rooks. Just after, follow it as it bends right heading for Bucklebury and ignore a turning left here, signposted to Stanford Dingley and Bradfield.

Follow the lane over a small brick bridge crossing the river Pang, after which the lane bends right. Leave the lane at this point and continue straight on, passing through a kissing gate and go across the centre of a field heading for the church of St. Mary, now directly ahead. At the far side, pass through a kissing gate, go over a gravel drive and then through a second kissing gate into the church yard. Follow a path through the church yard and note as you go, a number of iron headstones. At the church, follow a path right which runs to the left of a cottage (to visit the church itself, then take a brick path left to arrive at the entrance).

Bucklebury (OS. 553709 Map 174) *has over the centuries always been regarded as the capital of the Pang valley. Even in its earliest days the village enjoyed a level of importance, taking its name from the Saxon princess, Burghild, who made her home here. The village really rose to prominence when Reading Abbey, which held the manor, built a house here for the Abbot. With the ascension of Henry VIII to the throne, came the dissolution of the monasteries and the King sold the manor to John Winchcombe, son of the famous tailor, Jack of Newbury.*

John Winchcombe demolished the Abbot's house leaving only the five fish ponds which had provided the monks with a daily supply of fresh fish. In its place, he started to build a magnificent Elizabethan mansion. Unfortunately, he died before the house was completed, leaving the final stages in the hands of his son.

The Winchcombe family went on to hold the manor of Bucklebury for over one hundred and fifty years until the early 18th century, when the last of the male line of the family died and the heiress, Frances, inherited the manor with her husband, Henry St. John. During those years, the Winchcombes had become one of the most important families in the country. Religiously loyal to the Royal family, they welcomed Elizabeth I to the manor for dinner and years later, attracted the less welcome attention of the Parliamentarians during the Civil War.

On inheriting the manor, Henry St. John went on to use his new found wealth to further his political career. The couple became famous for throwing lavish parties and entertaining influential people of the day. Amongst the more famous of these, were Dean Swift, Alexander Pope and it is said, even Queen Anne herself. Henry St. John's career blossomed. He went on to become Secretary of State and in 1712, was made a Viscount, becoming Lord Bolingbroke. Unfortunately, this success was short-lived and three years after being made a Viscount, he was forced to flee to France to avoid impeachment. His marriage with loyal Frances had for years before been on shaky ground, mainly due to his flirtatious nature. In France, he committed the ultimate insult when after using his wife's inheritance to obtain most of his success, he openly rejected her by moving in with a wealthy French widow. Frances was devastated and died three years later in 1718, it is said, from a broken heart. Her ghost is reputed to roam the village in a coach pulled by four black horses.

The manor house sadly burned down in 1830 and had to be demolished. Only one wing was partially saved and this continues to form part of the manor house today. The fish ponds from the original manor built by the monks of Reading Abbey all those years ago, also remain.

The village church of St. Mary the Virgin, preserves the memory of those who have moulded village life over the centuries. The Winchcombes, as one would expect, are most prominent. Engraved on a wooden beam above the chancel, are the words "1591 Francis Winchecom Esquier Build This". The chancel also has a small annex which was added in 1705, probably by the then Henry St. John, to have a pew for his family and guests. The annex has a small stained glass window which doubles as a sundial and has the painting of a very realistic fly, indicating how time flies. The painter achieved such realism by painting the fly's body on one side of the glass and its wings on the other. Also, in the chancel on the floor, is a memorial to the tragic Lady Frances Winchcombe.

The church itself is Norman and still retains its magnificent south doorway with ornate carvings of flowers and faces. Sadly, it is often locked. If you do visit and find the door open, do not pass up the opportunity to explore one of Berkshire's most interesting churches.

Leave the church yard via a small wooden gate and follow the lane ahead, ignoring another lane right signposted to Stanford Dingley. Stay on the lane for some distance and after the last house on the left, "Waven" which often has honey for sale, take a signposted bridleway left to follow a track along the left hand perimeter of a field. After approximately twenty metres, the field perimeter bends gently right. You should leave the track here to continue straight on along a bridleway which runs between banks. This is very easy to miss, so take care. The bridleway continues uphill, along the slopes of the Pang valley. At first the route is guided by steep banks. Further up, these disappear and your route passes through a strip of woodland before continuing through open scrubland, a result of the infamous storm of 1987.

It is not long before the path enters woodland once again and continues the climb, now more steeply, out of the Pang valley. Are your legs hurting yet? You should ignore any turnings off to the left or right to eventually arrive at a more prominent track where there is a gate on your left - a convenient place to stop for a rest and enjoy the views back over the Pang valley and Bucklebury. After a short rest, go straight on along the track and pass a pretty cottage, "Vanners", on your right. Soon after this, the track enters woodland once more, the beginning of Bucklebury Common.

Bucklebury Common *covers an area of five square miles. Preserved by the ancient commoners rights, the common is a delightful, natural jewel in which bracken, heather and gorse thrive alongside a graceful scattering of birch. In the Civil War, Oliver Cromwell was said to have used the ample cover of the common to camp his army of twenty thousand men before the second Battle of Newbury. Time changes little and the common was used again in a similar fashion during the Second World War.*

For years the common supported a way of life, now all but extinct. Domestic animals roamed the common preserving its environment and maintaining a living for their owners. The abundance of trees brought skilled carpenters from miles around and the common became a centre for wood turning. In 1835, the common's finely balanced existence was threatened when Parliament looked set to enclose the common to prevent the straying of cattle. Thanks were due to a local preacher and farmer, John Morton, who travelled to Parliament and successfully opposed the threat. Sadly and to our loss, the way of life John Morton fought so hard to defend is all but gone. In its place, the common has become a rare haven for our threatened wildlife. Walking stealthily and keeping your eyes peeled, could well reward you with sightings of some of the inhabitants of the common.

You should ignore a crossing track at this point and carry straight on, thereafter ignoring any minor paths to the left or right.

The track continues through ancient woodland and after some distance, passes a lovely wooden barn on the right, now part of a residential property. Just after, you should leave the track and take another track which runs diagonally left. Take care not to miss this **(OS. 551692 Map 174)**. Again, you should ignore any turnings off and continue until you eventually meet a crossing track. Turn left here and stay on the track which, after a short distance, becomes concrete and follow it to later meet a lane. Cross the lane and join a track the other side, signposted as a byway and continue to soon meet a "T" junction. Bear left here along a track which follows a line of electricity pilons and is bordered by rough banks which have been created to ensure the so-called new age travellers continue travelling.

Go over a crossing track which is in fact a drive way to a house on your left and continue ahead. Sometime later, a house and some fields will come into view on your left and just after, the track will fork. You should take the left hand track to continue straight on and shortly after, go over another crossing track, also a drive way to a house. The track you are on soon joins a more prominent track coming in from the left, which you should follow to continue your route ahead. Soon after, go over yet another crossing track.

Sometime on, another track joins from the left and you should maintain your route ahead, passing a cluster of houses on your left, the hamlet of Scotland. You should still be following the line of electricity pilons referred to when we joined the track. As the hamlet ends, the track bends left and you should leave it and continue straight on along a less defined track, more a path. Again, this continues to follow the electricity pilons mentioned.

Eventually, the green at Chapel Row will come into view and ahead of you, the cottage from where the walk started. On reaching the green, turn right to reach "The Blade Bone Inn", our starting point and a welcome place to end - as long as you have returned during licencing hours!

ACCOMMODATION

The Six Bells, Beenham. Tel: 0734 713368
Two miles from the walk, accommodation is in a traditional 18th century village pub, complete with welcoming open fires in winter. The rooms, all en suite, have been tastefully decorated and afford open views over farm land. You may well hear wolves howling at night, but don't worry, they are bred by a local resident and are quite friendly.

Boot Farm, Bradfield. Tel: 0734 744298
Virtually on the walk, accommodation is in a comfortable Georgian house surrounded by a large and well kept garden. If you want to continue living the magic of the Pang valley, then Boot Farm is a must.

Ducarts, Stanford Dingley. Tel: 0734 744291
On the walk, returning to this lovely 16th century black and white beamed cottage after a day's walking in the Pang valley is a perfect end to a hopefully, perfect day.

Youth Hostel, Streatley YHA, Streatley. Tel: 0491 872278
Approximately eight miles from the walk, Streatley hostel now offers small family rooms as well as the normal dorms we all know. The hostel itself is a large Victorian house only a few paces from "The Bull" pub.

Camping and Caravanning, Dymond Farm, Shaw. Tel: 0635 47023
Approximately five miles from the walk, this is a small and peaceful site in a pleasant valley just north of Newbury. Facilities are good for such a small site, i.e. toilets, showers, etc. However, this does not detract from the rural aspect of the site.

IN GIANTS' FOOTSTEPS

Distance: 11¾ miles (19 km)
Time: Allow approximately 6 hours
Map: Ordnance Survey Landranger Map 174

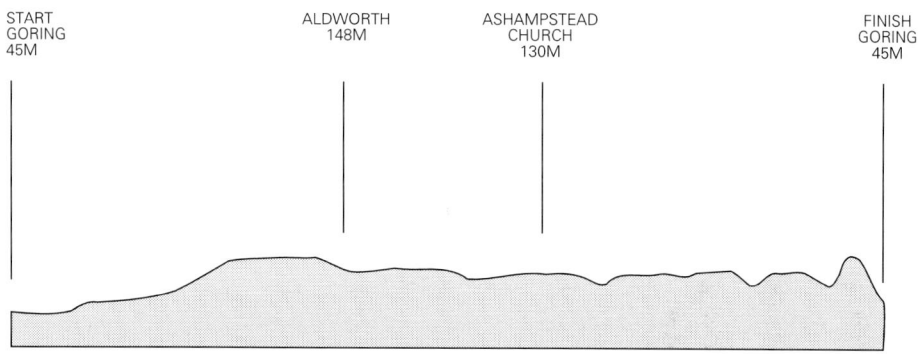

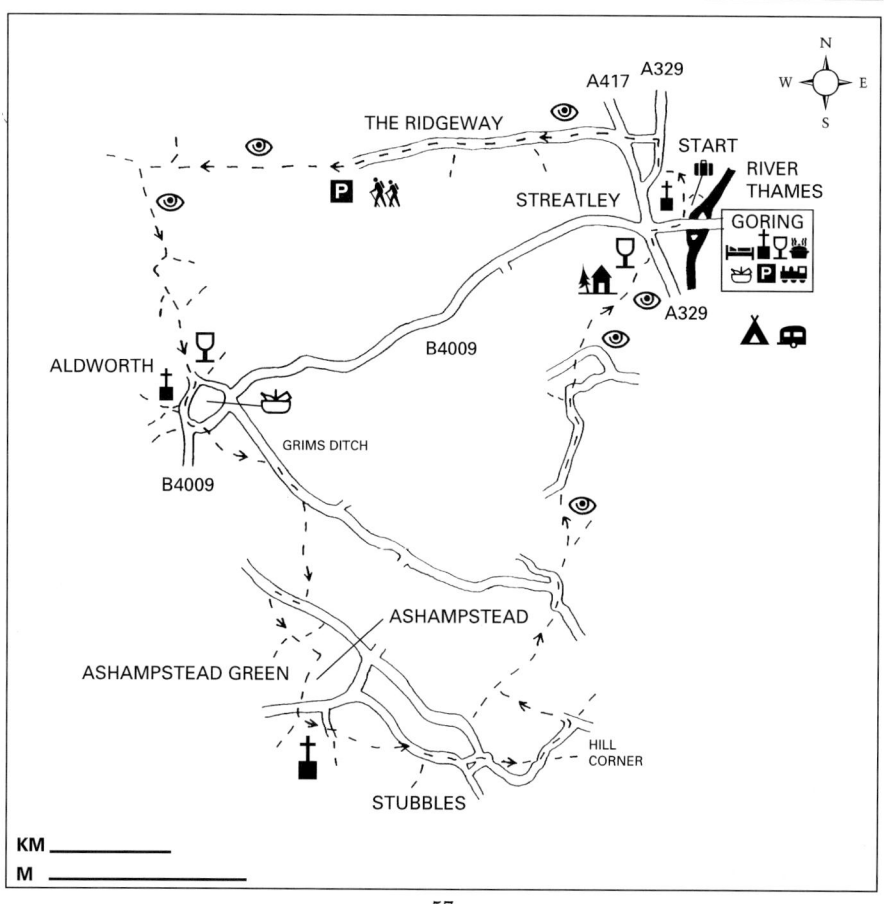

IN GIANTS FOOTSTEPS BERKSHIRE

| START GORING 45M | ALDWORTH 148M | ASHAMPSTEAD CHURCH 130M | FINISH GORING 45M |

Walk Summary
In Giants' Footsteps explores the tightly rolling hills west of the Goring Gap. The start of the walk follows the ancient Ridgeway over Thurle Down, with the reward of superb views back towards the Thames valley. After this, the route takes you up and down hills, much of it through typical English woodland, with a spectacular finish over Streatley Down with its famous views (if the mist stays away) over the Goring Gap.

The going can be muddy in places, even in summer, and the route has more than its fair share of ups, the hardest one being right at the finish, so do not treat it as an afternoon stroll or your may not make it.

Start - OS. 594808 Map 174
The walk starts from the start of the drive to the church at Streatley. If coming by car from the south and east, the easiest route is via the A329. You can either join this at Reading or by taking the A340 from the A4, just west of junction 12 on the M4. Follow the A340 to Pangbourne and turn left onto the A329 in the direction of the signs for Streatley. On reaching Streatley, turn right at the traffic lights in front of "The Bull" pub. There is parking either side of the road, the High Street, though please respect the residents' privacy and access.

If coming from the north, it is best to first make your way to Wallingford and from there to take the A329 south. On reaching Streatley, turn left at the traffic lights in front of "The Bull" pub, to park in the High Street. From the south east, the most direct and prettiest route is via the B4009 from Newbury. Follow this winding road all the way to Streatley. People living in nearby Buckinghamshire can best get to Streatley via Goring.

An alternative start can be made from a small car park on the Ridgeway near "Warren Farm" (OS. 567812). The nearest railway station is at Goring, the other side of the Thames. From there it is only a short stroll to join the walk. The station is on the line that connects Oxford with Reading and trains are fairly frequent.

IN GIANTS' FOOTSTEPS

It is not often that a walk starts from such pleasant surroundings, but at Streatley we are spoilt without effort. The only down side, is that many other people also recognise Streatley's charms and in summer especially, the streets can be crowded with people seemingly nervous to explore further than the High Street.

Streatley (OS. 594808 Map 174) *is at one of the most famous and oldest crossroads of Europe, for here the ancient Icknield Way and Ridgeway converge to cross another major highway, the river Thames. The waters of the Thames were before man started building weirs and locks, particularly shallow at this point and presented the only safe crossing for miles. Consequently, Streatley became a place of some importance and witnessed people both friendly and hostile, as successive races battled to control the thoroughfare. Today the surrounding countryside is littered with remains from the various Celtic, Roman, Saxon and Danish armies.*

Before the Romans, crossing the river meant fording it. The Romans built a causeway which carried their road or strata, from which Streatley derives its name. The causeway typical of Roman engineering, remained in use until the 17th century, when the more important requirements of river traffic lead to the building of the first lock. After this, the only way across the river was by ferry which was by all accounts, unsafe and unreliable. A tragedy in 1674, saw almost fifty people drowned when the overcrowded ferry capsized. Despite this, the first bridge was not built until 1838. The bridge in use today replaced the original in 1923.

It is a pleasant walk across the bridge to Goring and Oxfordshire. From the bridge itself you gain the best view of the two villages. On the Streatley bank is the smart "Swan Diplomat Hotel", the ornamental barge moored outside once belonged to Magdalen College, Oxford. On the Goring bank sits the old mill and a medley of boathouses. Below you, flow the timeless waters of the Thames, sedate around the lock and fierce beneath the weir. Fans of "Wind in the Willows" will recall how Rat and Mole first encountered the scene, described by Kenneth Grahame as, "the silvery shoulder and foamy tumble of a weir, arm in arm with the restless dripping mill wheel".

Walking back up the main street at Streatley past pleasant period houses, brings you to "The Bull Inn". This attractive pub dates from the 16th century and was a coaching inn on the main Oxford to Reading road, yet another major highway passing through Streatley. "The Bull Inn" is a free house and when I walked the Ridgeway path back in the late 1970's, it was a truly local pub. Nowadays, the inn has gone for the family trade in a big way and large signs advertise good value meals and extended opening hours. "The Bull Inn" has however, kept its cosy charm and is a warm place to relax after a day in the hills. The food too is good value and if you prefer to stay outdoors, it has a secluded garden.

Spoilt for choice, there are four other alternatives for refreshment. One is the "Swan Diplomat Hotel", though the interior does not allow for perspiring walkers in muddy boots. Much more down to earth is "The Miller of Mansfield" in Goring. This is a Courage pub, much photographed from the outside and not disappointing inside. It also doubles as an hotel. The best two hostelries, in my opinion, are to be found amongst the back streets of Goring off the southern side of the main street. They are "The John Barleycorn" and "The Catherine Wheel", both Brakespeare's pubs. Goring also has a number of tea rooms and cafes and for those who prefer eating in the hills, there is a general stores from which to buy provisions.

Two words of warning, although attractive the Thames is dangerous particularly beneath the weir and people are found drowned here all too regularly. Please treat the river with respect. Secondly, the inns at Streatley and Goring are all equally attractive, but remember there are almost twelve miles of hill walking to go and believe me, it is far easier on two legs rather than on all fours!

To start the walk itself, make your way to the church. The church like so many in Berkshire, is essentially Norman with heavy Victorian renovation.

✝

Inside there are some well preserved brasses. Facing the church entrance, follow the drive which bears right around the church to run between the church on your left and the "Swan Diplomat" hotel on your right. Shortly after passing some houses, the footpath forks and you should take the left hand fork, still following the drive and also marked as a footpath. Pass to the right of a water treatment plant where the drive narrows into a path and continue to arrive at a lane beside a play area on the left.

Turn left along the lane which is lined by horse chestnuts, to shortly meet a main road, the A329. Turn right along the A329 and follow it until you meet the first road on your left, signposted as Townsend Road. Take this which leads uphill to reach another main road, the A417. Turn left along the A417 for approximately fifty paces and then right onto a lane, Rectory Road, signposted to Goring and Streatley Golf Club and also marked as the Ridgeway.

i **The Ridgeway** *is an official long distance path or trail. It was opened in 1973 and stretches eightyfive miles from Overton Hill in Wiltshire to Ivinghoe Beacon in Hertfordshire. The route follows in the main, reputedly the oldest road in Europe and from here until you leave the Ridgeway, you are following a track which has seen constant use since the stone age. From the south coast, the original Ridgeway passed through Dorset to Stonehenge and then along a chalk ridge to eventually cross the Thames at Streatley. Thereafter, it continued in the form of the Icknield Way to Grimes Graves in Norfolk (neolithic flint mines) and on to the coast. When the track was in its earliest period the English channel did not exist and it is probable that from both coastlines it extended to the Continent. This would explain in particular, the similarity of the neolithic and bronze age remains in Brittany and those along the Ridgeway. It would also account for the vast amount of trade which the Ridgeway is known to have carried. Successive archeological digs have uncovered goods which have come from as far away as Egypt.*

Apart from a trading route, the Ridgeway also connected several important religious monuments including Avebury and Stonehenge. With the coming of the Celts hill forts were also built along the route. As time progressed, people gradually deserted the hills to inhabit the more sheltered and well watered lowlands. However, the Ridgeway remained a popular route, being easier to traverse than the often mud clogged lowland routes. Today, it is fitting that it has been turned into a long distance path. Preserved from the ravages of the motor car, walkers can experience Britain in the same way as the Ridgeway's earliest users and hopefully appreciate what so many have forgotten.

You now follow Rectory Road almost to its end, a distance of approximately one and a half miles, ignoring all turnings off. As you walk you will enjoy open views in places on your right and later pass the entrance to Streatley Golf Club on your left. There are a number of attractive properties en route, in particular "Thurle Grange" on the right.

You leave the lane when it eventually forks in front of a postbox and sign for "Warren Farm". Take the right hand fork, a track running uphill, signposted as the Ridgeway. The track climbs steadily uphill, in places being very muddy through the use of four wheel drive vehicles. To avoid the worst of this at the start of your climb, there is a narrow footpath running parallel on your left through the trees, which you may prefer to follow. There are lovely views as you climb to your left over a picturesque valley and "Warren Farm" itself nestling at the centre. The farm is home to a ghost, a woman who is said to roam the valley in her night dress. A shepherd witnessing the ghost believed it to be his lost wife and created such a fuss that an investigation was launched. A subsequent search uncovered a shallow grave in which the body of a blond haired lady was found. There have been no reports of recent sightings, but you never know.

On nearing the top of the hill look out for a gap in the hedge on the left, where you may wish to pause and take in the views. Below in the heart of the valley lies a distinctive clump of trees, with the valley itself ending abruptly by way of a steep slope at its head known as Streatley Warren, which rises to join the Berkshire Downs. At the other side of the valley is "Bower Farm". As you continue,

On the Ridgeway

ignore a track coming in from the left and soon after a marked footpath joining from the right. Stay on the Ridgeway until you eventually meet a track off to the left signposted as a byway. Take this thereby leaving the Ridgeway, and follow the track heading west towards "Bower Farm".

The track takes you across the head of the valley with views left back over your walk so far and beyond, to the Thames valley. As you near "Bower Farm", follow the track as it bends suddenly right and ignore a signposted byway at this point off to the left. Continue along the track to meet a "T" junction beside the entrance to "Bower Farm". This is the highest point on the walk, but before you cheer it is not the hardest climb! Turn left along a narrow lane and follow this for some distance enjoying your first views west. Ignore a track off to the right and later a signposted public footpath left and stay on the lane which now gradually descends. Ahead now, the rooftops of Aldworth village will come into view.

Follow the lane into the village until the it forks in front of a 19th century (1864) methodist chapel, now a private residence. Our route is along the right hand fork continuing through the village. First though, I recommend you pay a visit to "The Bell Inn", a traditional and unspoilt free house and the last hostelry before the finish at Streatley. To visit the inn take the left hand fork. The inn stands opposite a small green and the old village well, still complete with cog wheels and protected by a small roof. A plaque on the well states that it was sunk in 1868 by monies raised in the parish. The mechanics to draw the

Entering Aldworth

water were very necessary as the well sank to a depth of three hundred and seventytwo feet, the deepest in Berkshire. This idyllic scene however, is not the main reason people visit Aldworth, that is the village church and the stone giants. To visit these you need to rejoin our route which is easily done.

From taking the right hand fork at the chapel, continue to meet a "T" junction in front of the village grocers, McQuhae's, and turn right to follow a lane away from the village, signposted to Compton and Hampstead Norreys. Continue along the lane and as you approach the village church, ignore a signposted footpath off to the right. A visit to the church is a must.

St. Mary's Church, Aldworth (OS. 554794 Map 174) *conceals some unique treasures. From the outside, the church apart from being particularly attractive, appears no different from any other village church of a similar size. However, once through the door everything changes. It is as though you have stumbled across a mausoleum for giants, for set in the walls and in between the pews lie nine huge stone* figures. Some lie on their backs, others rest on their elbows and hips gazing across the body of the church.

The stone giants are the tombs of the Flemish de la Beche family who held the manor up until the mid-14th century. They lived not half a mile away in a castle now long gone but remembered in name by a farm and the present manor house which now occupy the site. During excavations at the farm, a fine silver seal was discovered. This was the seal of Isabella de la Beche and helped to prove the identity of the stone giants which are unmarked. There was at one time a parchment in the church with a plan of the tombs. Unfortunately, this was removed by Robert Dudley, Earl of Leicester, in 1644 when he brought Queen Elizabeth I to view the giants.

One of the most impressive giants is that of Sir Philip, easily recognisable by his huge size and the dwarf squatting at his feet. Sir Philip was valet to Edward II and at over seven feet tall, must have been an awesome figure at Court. To emphasise his stature he kept a dwarf as a servant who always accompanied him whilst on official duties. Edward II later appointed Sir Philip Sheriff of Berkshire and Wiltshire. However, Sir Philip repaid this favour by plotting to overthrow the King and led a rebellion in 1322 with Thomas, Earl of Lancaster. This treachery was not as bad as it at first appears, as Edward II was a weak King and easily manipulated. Sir Philip, along with others, often feared for the safety of the nation and despised the corrupt Court the King held.

The rebellion and consequential civil war was short lived coming to an abrupt end at the Battle of Boroughbridge in Yorkshire. Thomas, Earl of Lancaster, paid by being beheaded. Incredibly, Sir Philip escaped the expected punishment being imprisoned instead and stripped of the manor. Sir Philip's luck stayed with him, for five years later Isabella of France, once Queen to Edward II who had fled back to her homeland, returned with her son and heir to the throne. This time, Edward II was successfully deposed and suffered a slow and painful death at Berkeley Castle. Isabella's son, now Edward III, remembered Sir Philip's earlier attempt to dethrone his father and restored Sir Philip to the manor at Aldworth.

The family remained in favour of Edward, for Philip's second son, Lord Nicholas whose stone effigy lies in the nave of the church, was appointed Constable of the Tower and custodian to Edward's first son, better known as the Black Prince. During his lifetime Lord Nicholas witnessed the start of the Hundred Years War, turned the manor house into a castle, enjoyed the defeat of the French at the Battle of Crecy, was thrown in prison for neglecting his duties at the Tower and, it is believed, was the man responsible for the unique memorials to his family.

The death of Lord Nicholas ended the male line of the de la Beche family and perhaps this was the reason that Nicholas built such a memorial to his forebears. Whatever the reason, the giants have ensured that the de la Beche name is never forgotten. Records show that the giants once numbered ten, with one being buried under a wall of the church. Locals nicknamed this figure as John Everafraid and legend has it that this member of the family had promised his soul to the devil if he was buried inside the church or in the church yard. There is now no trace of his remains. The other nine giants are sadly in a poor state, many having broken limbs, a deliberate act of vandalism by Cromwells troops. Three of the giants were once known locally as John Long, John Strong and John Neverafraid, though which three I cannot tell you. Today, they are collectively known simply as the Aldworth Giants.

Outside the church are some more surprising memorials. A large tomb enclosed by railings is that of the parents of Emily Sellwood, wife to the poet Lord Tennyson. The Sellwood family lived at "Pibworth Manor" on the road to Compton. Tennyson so loved Aldworth that he named his house on Black Down in West Sussex after the village. The ashes of another poet, Laurance Binyon, are buried by the beech hedge which encloses the church yard. Binyon is most remembered for his poem "For the Fallen", now an essential part of the Rememberance Day services. Older than the church by several hundred years is the stump of an old yew. This once proud tree was sadly blown down in the infamous hurricane of 1987.

From the church yard there are magnificent views across the rolling Berkshire countryside. Visible are several farms but which one, I wonder, gave its name to Aldworth, Saxon for "old farm"?

Leaving the church, ignore a signposted byway leading to "Dumworth Farm" on the right and continue along the lane to meet a triangular green. Take the lane to the left of the green to meet the B4009 onto which you should turn left. Pass "Parsonage Green" on your right and thereafter, "Downland Cottage" and as the road bends left, take a track off to your right, signposted as a byway and initially tarmacced.

Follow the byway to soon pass a number of properties, the last one being a large house on the right called "Fayleys". Here the track changes to become more of a farm track and leads gently downhill through a beech wood. It later rises gently to arrive at a narrow lane onto which you should turn right. (If you wish to avoid lane walking, you can follow a narrow path parallel to the lane on your left which meanders through the beech trees). The lane soon passes through a bank and ditch, an ancient earthwork known as Grims Ditch.

Grims Ditch (OS. 562788 Map 174) *is one of several similar earthworks in the area. They are mostly of Celtic origin and it is believed, acted as boundaries often stretching for hundreds of miles. The name "Grim" is given to many ancient earthworks (remember Grimes Graves mentioned earlier), and is associated with the devil and also represents Woden, the Norse God, God of Warriors. Today, the bank and ditch are quite hard to spot, unlike their original appearance when together they could measure tens of feet.*

i

You should ignore any tracks leading into the wood on your right and continue along the lane until the wood virtually ends at the start of a field. Take a grass track right at this point, signposted as a public footpath. This winds through a mixture of deciduous and fir woodland and is also bordered by a mass of brambles which may be somewhat treacherous in summer. It then begins to descend where the going can be very muddy and slippery and later passes between two wooden posts to arrive at a large clearing. Go straight across the clearing, ignoring a track off to the left and continue ahead along a now very prominent track through a young plantation.

Ignore all turnings off and continue until the track bends sharp right just before reaching a lane. To follow the footpath proper, you now need to scramble down a steep bank to the lane itself, where you should turn right to follow the lane. Alternatively, you can follow the track which runs parallel to the lane and meets it further on - a much easier approach. The choice is yours, however, remember continuation along the track is not an official public right of way. Either way, you should follow the lane right for a few hundred metres, until you meet a signposted footpath on your left leading across a field.

Follow the footpath across the centre of the field in the direction of the footpath sign to meet the edge of a wood the other side. Bear left to follow the edge of the wood on your right, following the field perimeter. Soon after, on meeting a younger part of the wood, the field perimeter bears left. You should leave the field at this point and join a narrow path right into the younger wooded area, walking away from the field. After approximately thirtyfive paces, the path forks and you should take the left hand fork, a very narrow path and at first not easily distinguished. This soon leaves the younger wooded area to enter more established woodland and you should ignore a crossing path to continue ahead. Your way should now be marked by white arrows on some of the tree trunks. This area is a beautiful carpet of bluebells in spring and is still very much untouched.

As you progress the path becomes more distinctive, albeit can be a little overgrown in places in summer. You should continue your direction and be guided by the white arrows. At the other side of the wood, you are reassured of your route by way of a public footpath sign. Here you should take a track ahead (left) to continue your route. Do not make the mistake of taking a track right which leads back into the wood. The track ahead follows a strip of woodland between fields and can be extremely muddy. As with previous tracks on this walk, this area allows access to four wheel drive vehicles. Again to assist your progress, there is a small footpath which runs parallel to the track and between the trees on your right.

You will soon arrive at a small cluster of houses known as Ashampstead Green (**OS. 564773**). Do not enter the hamlet but on passing the first bungalow on your right, turn right into a small clearing before a double garage and take a narrow footpath to the right of the garage. The footpath leads away from Ashampstead Green through another strip of woodland, predominant in holly bushes and trees. It eventually leads out to a track, where you should carry straight on to reach a lane. The lane itself is very reminiscent of France, being straight and bordered by an avenue of limes. The other feature here is that of the land itself, now very flat and open, somewhat different to the earlier stages of our walk.

Cross the lane and join a concrete farm track ahead, signposted as a public bridleway and to "Casey Fields Farm". After approximately one hundred metres, go over a stile on your left into a field. Go straight across the field heading for the church ahead and at the far side, go over another stile to cross a smaller field. Cross a second stile into the church yard and continue to reach the main door of St. Clement's church.

St. Clement's Church and Ashampstead Village (OS. 564768 Map 174). *St. Clement's, like the church at Aldworth, has a surprise for those who venture inside. However, this time it is not stone giants but a number of colourful 13th century wall paintings which hold your attention. The complete 13th century nave and original narrow lancet windows enhance the scene, allowing you to imagine if only for a moment, that you are in another time. The paintings, it is believed, were the work of monks from Lyre Abbey in Normandy, who are also thought to have built the church. The best preserved paintings are on the north wall, they show the Annunciation (the proclamation of the angel to the Virgin Mary, now remembered as Lady Day, 25th March), the Visitation, the Nativity and the angel appearing to the shepherds. In the background can be seen a star and crescent. This was the badge of Henry III, who once had a hunting lodge at Ashampstead. Opposite the entrance is a poorer painting* *of St. Christopher, which was positioned in order that travellers could enter for a quick blessing with the minimum of delay to their journeys. Hints of modern living don't you think?*

Outside the church, like Aldworth, is the stump of an ancient yew. This one however, is quite dead and is unusual in that it is actually built into the north west corner of the church. Local tradition states that it was under this tree that services were held before the village had its own church and in memory of this the tree was incorporated into the building. If Ashampstead had no permanent church before St. Clement's, it is also possible that the part preservation of the yew was a compromise between the Christian church and the local population who probably still held strong pagan beliefs. These beliefs would have included the worshipping of the yew which was sacred in their eyes, the yew being the main protector of any village, warding off evil spirits. In the Church's battle to have Christianity accepted by the pagan Britons, they often compromised, one of the most common being the planting of a sacred yew in church yards. A yew tree older than the church nearly always indicates the site of an earlier church or a site once sacred to pagan worship.

The Church also allowed other compromises. One was to permit pagan festivities to be held in the church yard, the most famous of these being the May Dance. Another was to accept dates of pagan significance for Christian celebrations and in some cases, even adopt the pagan name. The most well known of these is Easter which is derived from the Saxon goddess, Eostre, the Goddess of Light. In 1285, the church attempted to curb the pagan influences and the Statutes of Winchester forbade the practice of holding pagan festivities in church yards. This was about the time of the building of St. Clement's. Could it have been that following this, the monks were bold enough to chop down the yew but were forced to keep the stump after public protest?

Before leaving Ashampstead it is worth exploring the village, the centre of which is left after leaving the church yard. There are a number of interesting houses, one "Blorenge House" (private), has in its garden a low brick tower with some external steps leading to the first floor. The tower was built in 1830 by a local preacher, Isaac Septimus Nullis, as a platform on which to practice his sermons. From the safety of the tower, it is said that Isaac would preach loudly to the farm animals grazing below until he had perfected his sermon.

From the church door, you should ignore the gravel path and bear gently right instead, to follow a grass path across the church yard. At the other side, go through a wooden gate onto a lane. Turn right along the lane for approximately fifty paces and then left onto a track, signposted as a public bridleway. The track runs along the left hand perimeter of a field and to the right of Ashampstead village green. Thereafter, it passes two small bungalows before continuing ahead between open fields. It later meets and follows a hedgerow on the left where as you progress, the hamlet of Stubbles comes into view.

On reaching the outskirts of the hamlet the track ends, twisting left to meet a lane. Do not join the lane but continue ahead along a narrow path at the edge of the field, which runs above and parallel to the lane. This meets the lane a little further on beside a track leading right which you should ignore. Turn right along the lane to walk through the centre of the hamlet taking care of any passing traffic. This soon takes you steeply downhill where the last building of the hamlet nestling at the bottom of the valley comes into view. This used to be a pub, "The Fleece and Feathers", but unfortunately, has recently been turned into a private residence.

As the lane forks, take the left hand lane to arrive at the house just mentioned and a crossroads. Go straight over the crossroads and join a small lane opposite, Whitemoor Lane, signposted to Quicks Green, which immediately goes uphill. As the lane bends right beside an old quarry, leave it and take a narrow signposted public footpath which winds uphill through woodland, known as Hanging Close Row. On reaching a track, cross this bearing gently left and continue along the footpath through more woodland. This route can in summer, in particular, be difficult to find and you may as an alternative wish to stay on the lane albeit a longer route to Quicks Green.

Follow the footpath through the woods and at the other side go over a stile into a field. Go diagonally right across the field heading towards some farm outbuildings on a hill ahead to your right. On nearing the field perimeter look out for a footpath sign, where you should cross a stile onto Whitemoor Lane. Turn left along the lane and follow it until it bends sharp right, where you should leave it to turn left onto a narrow lane marked as a dead end.

Follow the lane, initially passing some pictureque cottages, to its end beside two magnificent properties, the second being a converted barn. Here, you should carry straight on to now follow a signposted bridleway gently downhill, a track which can be very muddy in wet weather. As the track later begins to descend more steeply, look out on your right for the start of a new field which sweeps across a valley. Turn right at this point up a small bank into the field and continue ahead along the right hand perimeter. The field sweeps away to your left into the valley bottom and your route follows a hedgerow on your right. Take great care not to miss the entrance into the field, as this is currently unmarked. If you reach the bottom of the valley where the track bends left, then you will have gone too far and should retrace your steps to find the footpath at the top of the field.

As mentioned, follow the field perimeter ahead and as this bends away to your right, continue straight on across the centre of the field in the direction of a yellow public footpath arrow. At the other side of the field the path enters Bowers Copse, a particularly attractive part of the walk passing mainly through silver birch and conifers. The footpath is well defined and you should stay on it ignoring any minor turnings off, to eventually arrive at a small parking area beside a lane (**OS. 584776**).

Bear left along the lane and as this bends left, leave it to join another lane ahead signposted to Southridge. After a short distance, this lane also bends left and you should leave it to turn right onto a signposted footpath, which runs along the right hand perimeter of a field. Across the fields to your right at this point is "Hook Ends Farm" and ahead to your right you can just see the Thames valley.

At the far side of the field, the path enters woodland and you should continue to follow it, descending steeply through the woods with fields visible through undergrowth on your right. Approximately two thirds of the way down, look out for a stone water marker and a footpath left, marked by a yellow footpath arrow. Take this, a less prominent path which runs through the centre of the wood and soon after, continue uphill through more dense woodland. This can be quite tough going in summer and protective clothing is a must.

You will eventually arrive at a small area of open hillside where you will gain lovely views back over the valley just traversed - it's also a good place to stop for a breather. Continue to the top of the hill passing another stone water marker and cross over a

66

stile ahead into a field. Go straight across the field along the left hand perimeter and at the far left hand corner bear left to leave the field by way of a stile beside a gate. You will immediately arrive at a lane onto which you should turn right.

Follow the lane to soon pass under some electricity pilons and continue to pass the entrance to "Bennets Wood Farm". After this, the road begins to descend becoming steeper as you go. It then bends right where you should ignore a signposted byway off to the left, to continue until the lane bends right again. This time you should leave it to continue straight on along a prominent but unmarked path which leads gently downhill through woodland.

The path descends more steeply and leads out into a field. The scene ahead will either bring cries of appreciation for it is a truly beautiful English landscape, or cries of despair depending on your current state of fitness. The field you are in drops into a narrow valley, at the bottom of which a number of houses compliment the landscape. Behind them and the reason for the cries of despair, rises the perfectly rounded, very impressive, but very steep Streatley Hill - and you've guessed it, our route is straight up the hill and over the top! First however, to make things even more painful, we must start at the bottom and to get there you should turn left to follow the field perimeter downhill to meet a lane.

Turn right along the lane for approximately thirty metres, ignore a farm track left and then turn left onto a signposted public footpath, just prior to a house complete with luxury conservatory and pond. The footpath runs between fences, going uphill, and bends right to follow the perimeter of the garden. After the property, go over a stile and follow the path to begin the steep ascent of Streatley Hill. I shall not ask if your legs are aching, but I am sure you will appreciate the words of a local poem:-

> "The air is clear, the day is fine,
> The prospect is, I know, divine,
> But most distinctly I decline,
> To climb the hill at Streatley."

Your ascent eventually ends at a stile which you should cross into a small wooded area. Before doing so however, I suggest you take time not only to recuperate but to enjoy the views back over your climb.

Immediately after the stile, ignore a narrow footpath off to the left and continue ahead across an area of open woodland, more like a common in appearance. Carry straight on keeping a fence on your right and ignore a stile on the same side. Follow the fence which soon bears gently right and continue to meet two stiles. Ignore the stile on your right and cross the one directly ahead to follow a fenced footpath bearing gently left. The path now begins a gentle descent through woodland where you should ignore a stepped path on your left.

You will soon arrive at open grass hillside and will immediately realise another reason why Streatley Hill is so famous. If the day is clear, you will be treated to one of the best views to be found anywhere along the Thames. Streatley and Goring beckon below with the Thames cutting through the famous Goring Gap, separating the Berkshire Downs from the wooded Chiltern Hills which continue to the horizon. The view makes all the hard work worthwhile, unless of course you have timed your walk on a day when the infamous Thames mist is out in force. If it is, dare I suggest you return and climb the hill on another day. The view is doubly enjoyable as you can see that there are no further hills between here and Streatley, indeed the going is all downhill. In places the descent is very steep and a slow, cautious pace is advisable unless you want to end in a heap at the bottom.

Go straight ahead to descend Streatley Hill and after what can seem an age of taking tentative steps downhill, the path runs for a short distance between houses before levelling out to meet a main road, the A329. Cross the road, turn left along the pavement and follow the A329, passing a Youth Hostel on your left. At "The Bull Inn" turn right and return to the centre of Streatley and our starting point.

ACCOMMODATION

The Miller of Mansfield, Goring. Tel: 0491 872829
Virtually on the walk, this is a much photographed hotel at the centre of Goring. It has a relaxed atmosphere and a good restaurant attached to a cosy bar. What more could you want?

The John Barleycorn, Goring. Tel: 0491 872509
Virtually on the walk, this is a lovely 16th century inn and a local pub of great character. Set in the side streets of Goring away from the busy High Street, it has an informal and friendly atmosphere which can become lively in the evenings. Most enjoyable.

Youth Hostel, Streatley YHA, Streatley. Tel: 0491 872278
On the walk, the recently refurbished Streatley hostel now offers small family rooms as well as the normal dorms we all know. The hostel itself is a large Victorian house only a few paces from "The Bull Inn".

Camping & Caravanning, Gatehampton Farm, Goring. Tel: 0491 872894
Approximately three quarters of a mile from the walk, this is an informal site on the bank of the river Thames. Facilities are minimal but then that is the beauty of its location. A pleasant walk takes you to the attractions of Goring centre.

COX'S CHOICE

Distance: 12¾ miles (20.5 km)
Time: Allow approximately 7 hours
Map: Ordnance Survey Landranger Map 175

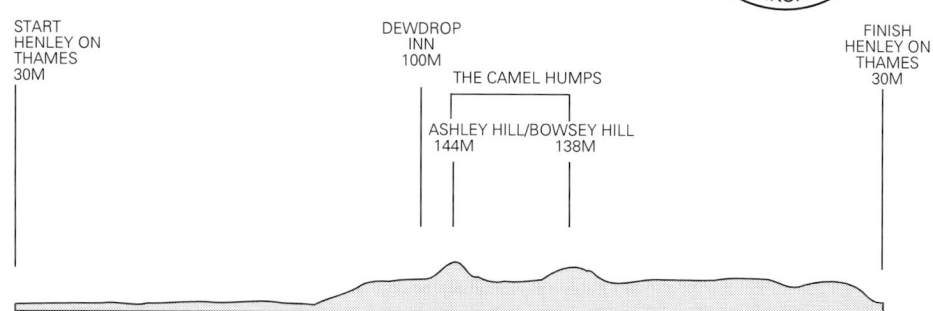

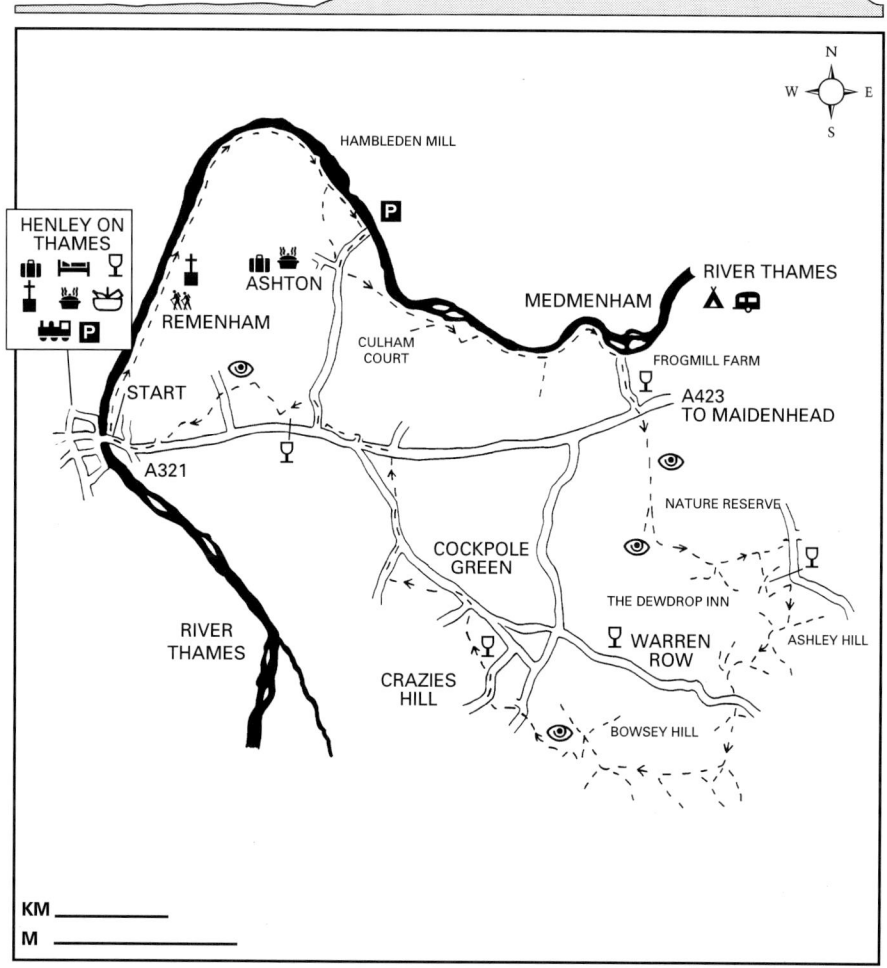

COX'S CHOICE
BERKSHIRE

START
HENLEY ON
THAMES
30M

DEWDROP
INN
100M

THE CAMEL HUMPS

ASHLEY HILL/BOWSEY HILL
144M   138M

FINISH
HENLEY ON
THAMES
30M

N
W   E
S

HAMBLEDEN MILL

HENLEY ON
THAMES

ASHTON

REMENHAM

CULHAM
COURT

MEDMENHAM

RIVER THAMES

FROGMILL FARM

START

A321

A423
TO MAIDENHEAD

NATURE RESERVE

COCKPOLE
GREEN

THE DEWDROP INN

WARREN
ROW

ASHLEY HILL

RIVER
THAMES

CRAZIES
HILL

BOWSEY HILL

KM _____
M _____

Walk Summary
This is a wonderful walk which discovers the delights of the Thames before exploring rolling fields and the wooded tops of Ashley and Bowsey Hills, which stand out like two camel humps on the south bank of the Thames. The walk is full of contrast as well as surprises, the most pleasant being "The Dewdrop Inn". Apart from "The Dewdrop Inn", there are several good hostelries en route, all conveniently situated. The going is fairly easy (unless the hostelries get the better of you!), with a couple of long but gradual climbs. There is though, being near a river, the familiar problem of mud so bring those boots. One word of warning, during the Henley Regatta the first part of the walk is closed. I therefore suggest you plan around the Regatta which starts on the second weekend in June and lasts for three weeks.

Start - OS. 764826 Map 175
The walk starts from the eastern side of the bridge at Henley on Thames, that is the side opposite Henley. Getting there is straight forward as Henley is served by several main routes. These are, the A321, the A423 and the A4155. Parking on the eastern bank is severely limited, so I suggest you park in Henley itself and walk across the bridge to start the walk. An alternative start can be made from the church at Remenham where there is limited parking (OS. 771842). Henley has a railway station which connects to a main line at Twyford.

COX'S CHOICE

From the eastern side of the elegant 18th century Henley bridge, facing away from Henley, take a drive on the left (north), passing between signs for Henley Royal Regatta. Immediately after joining you will see two footpath signs. You should take the left hand tarmacced path which runs between properties, the house on the right being the Leander Rowing Club, to shortly arrive at the river's edge. The Leander Rowing Club is of world renown, its members being selected not for their social standing but purely on their ability to row. Many of the best university oarsmen are members of the club.

Follow the river bank ahead by way of a tow path, with lovely views left to Henley and in particular the princely Edwardian boat houses. Behind them stands the tower of the famous Henley Brewery, brewers of the excellent Brakespeare's ales, which I have ensured you will have the opportunity to sample later on the walk. On regatta days, the grass area to your right here houses the hospitality and VIP tents, many of which are hired by the numerous rowing clubs based at Henley. It is not uncommon therefore, whatever the day, to see people rowing and training on the Thames.

i **The Henley Royal Regatta** *takes place on the longest reach of the Thames, though this is no accident, the river's course having been altered slightly. The first race which was also the beginning of the Oxford and Cambridge University races, was held in 1829 with Oxford winning. Then, the race started at Hambleden Lock and finished just beyond Henley Bridge. Ten years later, the Regatta was established and with the Prince Consort's patronage it acquired its Royal status. The start of the races then changed to Temple Island from where the races still start today. An unlikely benefactor to rowing history must be the railways. Before their intrusion into the Thames valley, the river was choked with barges transporting all manner of cargo. Travelling upstream, these barges sometimes required as many as fourteen horses to pull them. Racing then would have been impossible and unwelcome, but with the railways came the demise of the slower river traffic and by the mid-19th* *century, competition rowing was one of the most popular sports in the valley.*

Continue ahead to later pass through a wooden gate and carry straight on along a now much narrower tarmac path, still following the Thames. On your right are a number of attractive properties and more rowing clubs, one being the Upper Thames Rowing Club. These soon give way to more open grassland along the river bank. Sometime on pass "Old Blades", a lovely property on the right easily distinguished by its clock tower. Thereafter, the buildings of Remenham village will come into view.

As you continue along the tow path look out for a red brick building on the far bank of the river, this is "Fawley Court". The impressive design of the building is complemented by a scenic channel from the river which leads up to the main lawn. The house was built in 1684 from designs by Christopher Wren. It is now the "Divine Mercy College for the Marian Fathers". Soon after, you will pass some farm buildings on the right and should then pass over a cattle grid. Should you wish to visit Remenham, then turn right here over a stile adjacent to a large farm gate to enter the village centre, marked by its picturesque church.

Our route however, is straight on still following the Thames to soon pass Temple Island with its distinctive folly in the centre flow of the river.

Temple Island (OS. 771848 Map 175). *The folly on Temple Island was designed by James Wyatt in 1777 to improve the view from "Fawley Court". It also doubled as a fishing lodge. The name Temple Island pre-dates the building. It is probable that there was once a Romano Celtic temple here. Today the folly has another use as the starting point for the many races held on this stretch of the Thames. As a result of this latter point, many of the locals know the island as Regatta Island.*

The views now across the river beyond the island are of the hills of Buckinghamshire which curve with the horseshoe cut of the river. The terrain as you progress becomes more natural and open with fewer properties in view.

Pass through a kissing gate and continue along the tow path which gradually becomes less defined. You should continue to follow the river bank and look out for another very grand house again on the opposite bank, "Greenlands". This magnificent white mansion was built in 1871 by Viscount Hambleden, better known to you and I as W.H. Smith. It now houses a management college. Thereafter, you will arrive at Hambleden Lock with its large weir and beautiful mill house in the distance. There is a footpath along the bridge over the weir to the mill house, should you wish to take a short detour.

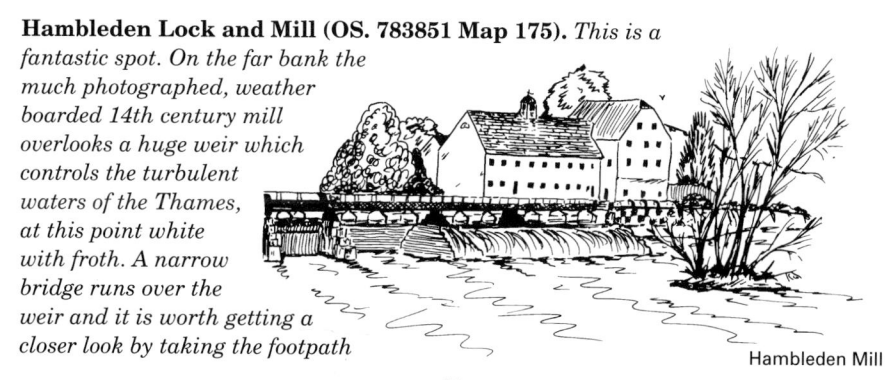

Hambleden Lock and Mill (OS. 783851 Map 175). *This is a fantastic spot. On the far bank the much photographed, weather boarded 14th century mill overlooks a huge weir which controls the turbulent waters of the Thames, at this point white with froth. A narrow bridge runs over the weir and it is worth getting a closer look by taking the footpath*

Hambleden Mill

across it to the mill. The total walkway is three hundred yards and allows for beautiful views of the river. I am sure I do not need to warn you, that the waters here are dangerous. Unfortunately, to confirm it, in 1753 a bargeman was killed here trying to shoot the weir.

The current mill was built in 1338, though there was one here even before this which was recorded in the Domesday Book. Today, the mill has ceased working but its future is preserved in the form of luxury apartments.

Our route continues along the right hand bank of the river, where the path graduates naturally into a prominent track. This soon bends right to go across fields, where you should leave it to go through a metal gate ahead into another field, thereby continuing your route along the river. Before you go any further however, it is worth stopping to enjoy the view back.

At the far side of the field, pass through a small wooden gate and go over a bridge to arrive at a parking area beside a sign for "The Flower Pot Hotel". Years ago, the Aston Ferry was based here taking passengers across the river to Hambleden Mill. Turn right and walk through the parking area and follow a narrow lane away from the river, which leads to the village of Aston and "The Flower Pot Hotel" itself - look out for the flower pot hanging outside the hotel acting as its sign. If you have started your walk early enough you may wish to take advantage of the fact that the hotel offers breakfast between 8.00 a.m. and 10.00 a.m. It is owned by the Henley Brewery mentioned earlier and specialises in fishing and boating parties. It serves excellent ales should your stop be a lunch time one, good food and offers a peaceful beer garden for a restful stop on a summer's day. One of my favourites!

On reaching a "T" junction beside the hotel, continue straight on bearing gently left along a wider lane and after approximately thirty metres, turn left onto a narrow tarmac lane. The lane bends right just after "Holme Farm" on your left, where you should leave it to carry straight on along a signposted footpath. After approximately forty paces, go through a kissing gate into a field and bear left to follow the left hand perimeter heading for "Culham Court", a large house visible ahead. You are rewarded at this point with superb views over the Thames on your left.

As the field perimeter bends away to the left, you should leave it to continue straight on across the centre of the field, still heading for "Culham Court". At the far side of the field, pass through a kissing gate and turn left to follow iron fencing on your right which leads around "Culham Court". Twenty paces on, pass through another kissing gate where you will now be directly in front of the house and its rolling lawns which lead down to the river's edge - another lovely spot.

Culham Court (OS. 789838 Map 175) *sits majestically above the Thames. From where we stand, wide steps lead up to its red brick frontage with well kept yew hedges concentrating the eye. The house dates from the 18th century and was restored in the 1930's. A famous tale from the house concerns George III, who whilst dining here insisted on having hot rolls from his favourite baker in London. The only method by which this could be achieved, was to transport the rolls by horse wrapped in hot flannels. Before the house was built, this part of the Thames through to Aston, was the scene of a ferocious battle during the Civil War. Today, such a battle could not be harder to imagine.*

Go through a kissing gate and continue ahead to leave the grounds by way of yet another kissing gate and enter a large field. Go straight across the centre of the field with views of the river on your left. At the far side, you will meet the perimeter fencing of a nursery, "Doorn Landscapes", on your left. You should continue ahead with the perimeter fencing on your left until you reach a kissing gate at the end of the field. Go through the gate to arrive at a gravel track.

Do not turn right but carry straight on in the direction of a public footpath sign, to immediately pass "Horns" on your left where the track becomes a farm track and runs between fields. After some distance, the track ends at a narrow tarmac lane where you should turn left passing through a kissing gate, in the direction of a footpath sign. The path initially follows perimeter fencing on your right, but as the latter ends you should follow the path as it bears diagonally right across the field.

At the far corner of the field, go through a kissing gate and over a wooden bridge into another field, where you are now back on the right hand bank of the river Thames. To your right, as a guide, are the buildings of "Lower Culham Farm". At the far side of the field, pass over an inlet by way of a small bridge with a stile at each end into another field. Continue straight on across the field still following the river on your left and at the field end, cross over a stile and another footbridge over a second inlet. Again, you should continue ahead along the river bank, ignoring a signposted footpath off to the right.

The field follows the curve of the river and at the far side, you should pass through a kissing gate and thereafter, bear left to reach the immediate bank of the Thames. There are lovely views across the river here to the hamlet of Medmenham.

Medmenham and the Hell Fire Club (OS. 806837 Map 175). *One of the houses at Medmenham looks suspiciously as though it was once an abbey. It is in fact a clever folly, though this folly is perhaps more genuine than most, as the materials used were taken from a ruined Cistercian monastery which once stood at Medmenham. The house to which the folly was added is Elizabethan and together they create an effective illusion. Sir Francis Dashwood thought so too and purchased the property in the mid-18th century.*

Sir Francis was notorious for creating the "Monks of Medmenham", better known as the infamous "Hell Fire Club". The club had forty-five members, all close friends of Sir Francis and many of them Members of Parliament, including the Lord Mayor of London, the First Lord of the Admiralty and the Treasurer for Ireland. Members of the club specialised in holding outrageous parties, better described as orgies. Twice a year, the club held what they called "full meetings", which were basically parties that lasted a week. On these occasions, it is said that members dressed up as monks and introduced ladies, dressed as nuns, who had to be of "a cheerful, lively disposition", to the group. All the ladies had to wear masks. The most memorable moments of these parties, Sir Francis had carved in stone and displayed them along the river frontage of the house, much to the annoyance of the local population.

The club held its meetings at Medmenham until 1763 when Sir Francis decided to move the club's activities to some spectacular caves beneath a hill at West Wycombe. On the hill above the caves he built a mausoleum with urns intended to hold the hearts of the members of the Hell Fire Club.

Today, all is peaceful at Medmenham and all signs of the Hell Fire Club, even stone ones, are gone.

Turn right and follow a now very narrow path through woodland along the river bank. The woodland quickly ends where you should cross a stile ahead and continue alongside the river, ignoring a gate on your right signposted as a bridleway. At this point, an island stands in the mid-flow of the river and there appears to be a greater frequency of ducks. The reason is soon apparent, for you shortly meet "River Barn", a large barn converted into luxury apartments on your right. Here we leave the river, turning right to join a drive in front of the barn.

Do not turn left, but follow the drive ahead past the barn and thereafter, "Frogmill Court" and "Frogmill Stables" and ignore another drive off to the right. Stay on the drive until you reach the A423 beside "The Black Boy" pub, Brakespeare's, which apart from excellent beer, offers accommodation and food. It also has a small beer garden. Turn left and pass in front of the pub and then cross the road to join a signposted public bridleway the other side.

The bridleway known as Hodgedale Lane, leads gently uphill between fields and is bordered by shallow banks which act as home to an abundance of rabbits. As you continue uphill, take time to stop and enjoy the views behind over the Thames valley. Note in particular, the distinctive grand white building on the north bank of the Thames. This is "Danesfield" (the name refers to an ancient fort occupied by the Danes), a Victorian mansion built for Robert Hudson whose family made their fortune in soap. The house is now an hotel and I am sure a clean one at that!

As you continue ignore a footpath off to the right. On nearing the top of the hill the bridleway becomes thick with hedges hiding any views back over the Thames. This area is also part of a small nature reserve run by BBONT (Berkshire, Buckinghamshire and Oxfordshire Naturalists Trust). The path soon meets a group of beech trees and here you should look out for a path on your left marked by a low stone marker, "Public Bridleway to Honey Lane". Take care not to miss it.

Take the bridleway which runs to the left of the beech trees and look out for the guiding white arrows painted on some of the tree trunks. After a short distance, ignore a stile off to the right, an entrance to the nature reserve, and continue along the bridleway to meet a gate. Go through this and follow a fenced path between fields, where you are immediately rewarded with excellent views across to Bowsey Hill on your right and ahead, to the wooded Ashley Hill.

Ignore a stile on your right and carry straight on heading for Ashley Hill. Pass through a metal gate and after approximately fifty paces join a concrete track and continue ahead. The track passes a small chalk quarry on the left which is hidden in the main by conifers. It then bends right where you should leave it to turn left onto another track, though not concrete, signposted as a footpath. The track runs in a straight line between fields heading for "Top Farm", with Ashley Hill now in the distance on your right.

As you approach the farm pass two rectangular ponds on your right and immediately after, turn right and pass through a wooden gate into a field in the direction of a bridleway sign. Go straight on along the right hand perimeter of the field and at the far side, pass through a wooden gate and continue ahead, ignoring two signposted footpaths on your left and right respectively. The view behind now is of the Buckinghamshire hills above the Thames valley.

Stay on the path which passes through a small strip of woodland and continue to arrive quite unexpectedly at a beautiful pub, "The Dewdrop Inn". This is another

Brakespeare's pub and one which requires a lot of will power to ignore. The long narrow bar has escaped alteration over the years and thus retains its original charm. The one problem with stopping here is that it requires even more will power to leave! For those who need to restock, "The Dewdrop Inn" serves some good bar food and in summer you may even be lucky enough to arrive when a barbecue is in progress.

From the pub, follow the driveway to meet a narrow tarmac lane. Turn left along the lane which follows the base of the wooded slopes of Ashley Hill and continue to meet another lane. Turn right here onto a signposted footpath and follow a track uphill heading for the summit of Ashley Hill. You should ignore any turnings off and on nearing the top, go over a crossing track to continue your route. The trees at the top of the hill are mainly deciduous with a sprinkling of pine.

The track eventually meets a "T" junction in the form of a semi-tarmacced drive. You should turn right along the drive and walk towards a house ahead, "Keeper's Cottage" (**OS. 824812**). At the property, turn right in front of the gates and after approximately twenty paces, turn left along a narrow footpath following the property perimeter. At the other side, you will meet a wider path onto which you should turn left. Through the trees here are views again over the Thames valley and as you continue, look out for the trig point in the garden on your left, marking the hill summit (144m) and the highest point on our walk.

Shortly after leaving the property behind, look out for a signposted footpath on your right which you should take. The path leads downhill through woodland which in spring is a mass of bluebells, snowdrops and daffodils. You should ignore a wide crossing track to continue your descent, where as you progress fields will come into view through the trees on your left. Approximately two thirds of the way down, ignore a path coming in from the right in front of some wooden rails and continue ahead to pass through the rails, still going downhill. There are marvellous views left across southern Berkshire to Finchampstead Ridges.

Pass over a stile, immediately after which you should ignore a signposted bridleway off to the right and twenty paces after, take a signposted footpath left. Follow the footpath as it winds through woodland gently downhill to eventually meet a lane. Cross the lane and continue ahead along a signposted footpath the other side. Go gently uphill and pass over a narrow crossing path to cross a stile into a field ahead. Turn right and follow the right hand perimeter for a few paces, to reach and cross a second stile beside a farm gate into the next field.

Go diagonally left across the field and as you reach the brow of the hill, head for a stile and gate at the far corner, just to the right of a house. As you progress across the field there are good views right of Bowsey Hill, our next destination. Go over the stile and turn left for approximately ten paces before turning right over a second stile into a field. There are two marked footpaths here. Our route is across the centre of the field, ignoring the path which follows the left hand perimeter. The buildings and area to your left form part of Knowl Hill, a village famous for being home to one of the largest steam rallies in the south of England. The steam rally is held on the second complete weekend in August and if you are in the area it is well worth attending, not just to admire the steam engines, but also to experience the huge beer tent which plays host to a number of small breweries.

At the far side of the field take time to stop and admire the views back. From here, on a clear day, it is possible to see the Chiltern Hills and even Windsor Castle. Go *i* over a stile just to the right of a small wooden gate to reach the base of the wooded slopes of Bowsey Hill. Turn left for approximately thirty paces and then right onto a signposted public bridleway. Follow the bridleway uphill, which at first passes a quarry on the left. Several years ago, this was used as a set for the films "The Land that Time Forgot" and "Journey to the Centre of the Earth". You need to keep to the bridleway, ignoring any turnings off including a signposted footpath left, until you reach the top of Bowsey Hill, signified by a large junction of tracks. The distance from joining the bridleway to the top of the hill is approximately one third of a mile. The hill is home to many deer, so keep your eyes peeled.

On reaching the junction of tracks mentioned (**OS. 809799**), turn right to follow a track along the top of the hill. After a short distance, you will meet a tarmac lane which you should follow ahead, passing a number of houses. Ignore a signposted footpath on the right and ten paces thereafter, turn left almost opposite "Hilltop Cottage" to go downhill, between houses, along a track. (Just before doing this

◉ however, if you continue on for a few paces to a parking area, there are marvellous views left across to western Berkshire and the North Hampshire Downs).

Returning to our route, follow the track downhill and look out on your left for a house with unusual twisted chimneys. After the last property on the right, continue straight on to meet a junction of paths and take a signposted footpath right to go over a stile. Follow the footpath, often muddy in wet weather, which runs behind the properties at the top of Bowsey Hill and continue to pass through a gap in a wooden fence. Thereafter, follow the footpath as it bends left away from Bowsey Hill summit and continue gently downhill to soon meet a crossing path. Turn right here and after approximately fifteen paces, go over a wide crossing track to continue ahead. After another twenty paces, the path forks and you should take the right hand path, through trees, marked by distinctive white arrows on the tree trunks.

The track you crossed earlier soon runs parallel on your right with the path you are following. After this, you should go over another crossing track and continue straight on, still following the white arrows, to meet the wide track on your right before bearing away again still in the direction of the white arrows. Take care to maintain your route at this point and use the white arrows for guidance and confirmation that your direction is correct. The wide track continues to run parallel with your route and later meets it again, this time crossing your path. You should continue ahead to meet a fork where you should take the left hand path, still in the direction of the white arrows.

The path runs diagonally downhill to then follow a stream on your right. (If you find yourself going steeply downhill and then crossing the stream, you will have taken the wrong fork and should retrace your steps). Follow the stream through the wood where a field will soon come into view on your right. Our route does not quite meet the field but continues through the wood and after a short distance, bends gently to meet a stile. Go over the stile and turn right along a lane and after approximately twenty metres, turn left onto a signposted public bridleway. The bridleway leads you through more attractive woodland where after a short distance, you are suddenly surprised at the appearance of a small ornate building, covering a muddy pool of water on your right. This is Rebecca's Well.

i **Rebecca's Well (OS. 799805 Map 175)** *looks as though it has been transported in one piece from Bavaria where such a feature is commonplace. The building acts as a cover for a spring preventing falling leaves and debris from polluting the water. The spring before the construction of its cover was known as "Phillimores Spring".*

Rebecca's Well

Phillimore was the local curate and it was he who built the basin at the spring's base which has an inscription from Chaucer and a cross. The gabled cover was built in 1870 and later the facia was painted. The painting depicts a scene from the Bible, Genesis 24, with Isaac, a servant of Abraham, begging Rebecca for a drop of water from her pitcher. Since the painting, the spring has been known as Rebecca's Well.

If you look carefully on the wall under the gable you will see many scratched inscriptions. These were written by the local population who put their hopes in what they believed was a wishing well. The spring was once the only source of water for the residents of Crazies Hill. Today, its only real value is its beauty, as looking at the colour I would certainly not recommend drinking the water.

Just after Rebecca's Well, ignore a signposted footpath off to the left and continue straight on along the bridleway to run between houses and continue onto a drive. Carry straight on to soon meet a lane onto which you should turn right and follow it gently uphill passing between some attractive properties which make up the village of Crazies Hill

Crazies Hill (OS. 799806 Map 175). *The name does not refer to the village inhabitants, but to the meadow buttercups which once grew in abundance on the hill. Years ago, it was believed that buttercups hung around the neck could cure lunacy, hence the name "Crazies". Unfortunately, modern farming methods have meant that nearly all the buttercups have gone, the meadow buttercup is poisonous to cattle and so many farmers actively destroy them.*

Pass the village hall, at the same time ignoring marked footpaths off to your left and right and continue past the magnificent "Summerfield House". Immediately after, take a signposted footpath left to reach and cross a stile into a field. There are two white arrows here and you should follow the path in the direction of the right hand arrow, which goes diagonally right across the field. After a short distance, follow the right hand field perimeter where there are excellent views ahead.

At the far right hand corner of the field pass through a kissing gate into another field and continue ahead along the right hand perimeter. Two thirds of the way across the field, look out for a stile on your right which you should cross into another field. Go diagonally left across the field along a distinctive path to the far corner. Go through a gap in the fence here to meet a lane. Turn left along the main lane (do not make the mistake of taking the smaller lane left here), in the direction of the signs for Remenham Hill, Henley and Hurley.

Pass "Ashley Hill Place" a new road off to your right and approximately twenty metres thereafter, go over a stile on your left into a field. Go diagonally right across the field where the landscape is markedly different to anything traversed in the earlier parts of the walk, the land being flat and very much exposed. Looking around, it is easy to see why the RAF used the fields here as a temporary airfield during the second World War. At the far side, go over a stile and continue ahead along the left hand perimeter of the next field. Follow the field perimeter round until you meet a kissing gate beside a larger gate. Go through the kissing gate onto a lane, opposite the entrance to "Pillar Lodge", and turn right along the lane, where to your right there are once again clear views across to Ashley and Bowsey Hills.

After a short distance, you will meet a "T" junction where you should turn left onto Culham Lane, in the direction of the signs to Remenham Hill, Henley and Hurley. At this point, be reassured that you are only two miles from Henley from where we started. Pass "Upper Culham Farm" and a number of pretty cottages and sometime later, the old blacksmiths. Just after this, take a track on your right which leads into a field. From here, you should follow the right hand perimeter of the field, in the direction of footpath sign. At the far side, cross over a stile to meet a main road, the A423. Cross the road and turn left along the pavement and on meeting a row of houses just before a sign for Aspect Golf Club and opposite Culham Lane, turn right onto a track beside the houses.

When the garden on your left ends, turn left to follow a narrow path running behind the houses on your left and adjacent to a field on your right. There are good views right here across to the hills beyond the river Thames. As the houses on the left end, turn left and follow the field perimeter round until you meet a lane, Aston Lane. Turn right down Aston Lane for a few hundred metres and opposite the last house on the right, turn left along a fenced footpath. Follow the footpath, ignoring all turnings off to eventually lead out onto a driveway.

On meeting the drive, follow this ahead to meet a gravel drive. Should you wish to take a rest in the form of a visit to a local hostelry, then turn left here to reach "The Seven Horseshoes", another Brakespeare's pub. Our route however, is right along a signposted footpath which runs to the left of the gravel drive. The footpath runs behind laurel bushes and soon bends away from the drive to run through pleasant deciduous woodland. Stay on the footpath, ignoring any minor turnings off, until the woodland ends where you should pass through a wooden gate into a field.

Bear gently left across the field and at the far side, cross over a stile into the next field, where again there are lovely views over the Thames valley. Go straight across the field to pass through a gate onto a lane. Turn left along the lane for a few paces and then right over a stile onto a signposted public footpath. Follow the footpath through mixed woodland for some distance, ignoring all turnings off. Sometime later, you should go over a crossing track and continue ahead for approximately twenty paces to meet a fork. Take the left hand fork which narrows as you go, running gently downhill.

The path then runs between iron railings where you will catch your first glimpses of Henley and passes a tennis court on your right. Thereafter, you will meet a drive which you should cross to continue your route downhill to eventually meet the A423. Turn right here along the pavement and follow the A423 downhill into Henley, our starting point. Just before you reach the bridge, you will pass two more excellent Brakespeare's pubs, "The Two Brewers" and the famous "Little Angel". Both are conveniently positioned should you feel you deserve one last reward before entering Henley - there are of course, even more pubs in Henley to reward yourself further!

ACCOMMODATION

The Flower Pot Hotel, Aston. Tel: 0491 574721
On the walk, this is the perfect place to stay. Set in tranquil surroundings the hotel is only five minutes walk from the river. The rooms are tastefully furnished and maintain the bygone character for which the hotel is well known. As mentioned in the text, the hotel specialises in fishing and boating parties.

The Black Boy, Hurley. Tel: 0628 824212
On the walk, this is a comfortable inn situated only five minutes walk from the river. The inn is easy to find being on the main A423.

The Two Brewers, Remenham. Tel: 0491 574375
On the walk, this is a simple and unpretentious local pub offering value for money and a lively atmosphere.

Youth Hostel, Windsor YHA, Windsor. Tel: 0753 861710
Approximately eleven miles from the walk, this hostel is in an attractive Queen Anne house in the village of Clewer (one mile west of Windsor). Accommodation is comfortable and the hostel is licensed to sell alcohol with meals. It can get very crowded in summer, so book ahead.

Camping & Caravanning, Hurley Caravan & Camping Park, Hurley. Tel: 0628 823501
A pleasant one mile stroll along the Thames from the walk, this is a large but enjoyable site on the south bank of the river. It has all the main facilities and although it can become crowded, the owners are careful to ensure the pitches are a good distance apart.

N.B. There is a wealth of accommodation at Henley on Thames. For a complete list contact the Tourist & Information Centre, Town Hall, Market Place, Henley, Oxfordshire (Tel: 0491 578034).

ESCAPING THE GALLOWS

Distance: 13 miles (21 km)
Time: Allow approximately 6 hours
Map: Ordnance Survey Landranger Map 174

START	WEST WOODHAY	AERIAL MAST	COMBE	FINISH
CAR PARK	HOUSE	COMBE HILL	177M	CAR PARK
WALBURY HILL	160M	287M		WALBURY HI
265M				265M

Walk Summary

This is a glorious walk of two distinct halves. The first half descends from the heights of Inkpen Hill to explore the pleasant pastures around Inkpen. A steep ascent of West Woodhay Down then transports you to the striking rolling hills surrounding the hamlet of Combe. If your energy fails, you can escape the second half by taking a short cut from West Woodhay Down. Most of the walk is fairly undemanding, though if you do do the full route, there is a long slow climb through Combe Wood and then to finish you off, a steep ascent right at the end. Parts of the walk are very muddy, especially around Inkpen, so come prepared.

Start - OS. 370620 Map 174

The walk starts from the Gibbet car park on the western side of Walbury Hill fort. If coming from the north east, take the A4 from Newbury and after five and a half miles, just after a turning for the Elcott Resort Centre on the the right, turn left onto a road signposted to Kintbury. This is opposite a turning to Wickham. Follow the road over the river Kennet and canal into the centre of Kintbury. From here, take a turning left, signposted to Inkpen, New Mill and Industrial Area. This is opposite the Corner Stores and is called Inkpen Road. Follow the road out of Kintbury until you meet a crossroads just after a pub on your left. Turn right at the crossroads, signposted to Inkpen, Ham, New Mill and Industrial Area. Stay on the road, following the signs for Upper Inkpen and on reaching a "T" junction, turn right in the direction of the signs to Lower Inkpen, Ham and Hungerford. Stay on the lane until you meet a crossroads. Turn left here following the signs for Combe Gibbet and Combe. Follow the road to the top of the hill, where, a lane leads off to the left. Here, also on your left, is a car park and our starting point. As a guide, Combe Gibbet is on the right.

If coming from Hungerford, from the High Street turn into Park Street beside "The Plume" pub, which is just south of the railway bridge. Continue and later turn right onto a road signposted to Inkpen and Combe and follow this, ignoring all turnings off, to eventually reach a "T" junction just after "The Swan Inn". This is also beside a small village green. Take the turning right signposted to Combe and Ham and continue to later take a turning left following the signs for Upper Inkpen and Combe Gibbet.

If coming from the south, take the A343 Andover to Newbury road and just north of Hurstbourne Tarrant, take a turning opposite a garage signposted to Netherton, Faccombe and Linkenholt. Follow the lane ignoring all turnings off to pass through Combe and shortly after arrive at the car park on the top of Walbury Hill.

The nearest railway station is at Kintbury. There is no obvious alternative start, although there is another car park on the eastern side of the hill fort should the Gibbet car park become full.

ESCAPING THE GALLOWS

The car park at Walbury Hill rewards without effort, magnificent views over the Kennet valley to the Lambourn Downs and to the south, the hills surrounding the hamlet of Combe. If you can read a map well, it is possible to trace your route through the surrounding countryside from here, though be careful that this does not put you off!

From the car park, head west to reach and cross a road and join a track the other side, signposted to Combe Gibbet, which runs along the top of Gallows Down. This track known as the North Hants Ridgeway, was an ancient neolithic trading route as was the more famous Ridgeway to the north of the county. It linked a series of hill forts in Wiltshire right through to those on the North Downs in Surrey. Today, the track is also used by four wheel drive vehicles and can therefore, be extremely muddy in wet weather. Its benefit however, is that it constantly affords excellent views.

After a short distance, you will pass a parking area and the famous gibbet of Inkpen Beacon. Here there is a stile you can cross should you wish to take a closer look.

Combe Gibbet (OS. 364623 Map 174) *has been a distinct and forbidding landmark since 1676. In that year it was errected to hang George Broomham of Combe and Dorothy Newman of Inkpen for the murder of Mr. Broomham's wife and son. On their capture, the authorities at Winchester (for Combe was then in Hampshire) refused to travel such a distance to try the pair. Instead, they paid the Berkshire authorities for their trouble. The pair were tried at Newbury and found guilty. Their end was at this gibbet where they were left to rot as a warning to other would-be murderers.*

The gibbet has never been used since, though a condition of the lease to "Eastwhick Farm" was that the gibbet be maintained. Today, this is done by public subscription, preserving the warning to locals and tourists alike. There are inevitably tales of shadowy figures haunting this spot. Just in case, I suggest you do not "hang around"!

The mound on which the gibbet stands was once a long barrow. This is a form of grave or burial ground used by neolithic man. The entrance would normally be from the east and large sarsen stones were used to create several chambers. The dead were cremated and their bones placed in clay beakers or urns along with their most prized belongings, usually jewellery or weaponry and placed in the chambers. The chambers were then covered in earth. This method of burial led these people to be known as "Beaker People". Like many other burial mounds in the country, this barrow is said to contain some hidden treasure. In this case, the treasure is a gold table and a curse dictates that death will come to anyone who tries to remove it.

Today, the long barrow and gibbet also mark the start (or finish) of two long distance walks, the Wayfarers Walk and the Test Way.

To continue our route, pass the gibbet following the track to later arrive at a junction of tracks. Turn immediately right here and go through a metal farm gate and follow a track, marked on the map as a bridleway, almost going back on yourself and passing a small dew pond on your left. After a short distance, bear left away from the track to reach the ridge of the hill. Continue ahead for approximately twenty metres, looking out for a narrow, unmarked and fairly undefined path on your left which runs directly downhill. This is marked as a bridleway on the map and as a guide, is opposite a small hollow at the top of the hill.

Take the bridleway steeply downhill, which runs between banks becoming more prominent as you go. Follow it as it bends left to follow the hill escarpment down. This is a very steep descent and you would have to be a brave rider to take your horse this way! On nearing the bottom of the hill and the end of a field, follow the bridleway as it bends sharply right and later passes a deep rectangular hollow on your left. This is just prior to a small wooden gate on the left and a signposted bridleway. Go through the gate and follow the bridleway as it bends almost immediately right. The bridleway, an old drovers road, is lined by hedges and trees and runs in a straight line heading north between fields. It has the wonderful name of Bungum Lane. This is a corruption of the French "Bon Hommes" and refers to the godly knights Hospitallers, who had their house here during the 12th century. The name also reveals the age of the path we are following.

The bridleway eventually meets a wider track, another bridleway, which you should follow to continue going straight on (do not turn left). This also runs in a straight line north, albeit not tree lined but between fields affording excellent views. Over to your near left is Inwood Copse and also the end of the Wansdyke, a huge earthen bank which stretches from here to the Bristol Channel. Its purpose was probably defence, but by whom and against what is still much disputed. Stay on the track for some distance to eventually meet a lane. On your right here, you can see the red tiled tower of Inkpen church. Turn right along the lane, passing a sign on your left welcoming you to Inkpen and soon after the lane bends right, turn right along another lane signposted to Upper Inkpen and Combe. Pass a lovely brick cottage on your left and shortly after, a large barn beside another attractive house on your right. Thereafter, ignore a signposted footpath on the left and continue along the lane passing the entrance to Inkpen church and "The Rectory" adjacent.

Inkpen Church (OS. 357638 Map 174) *is well worth a short stop. Humble in appearance, it nestles below the grander rectory which was built in 1695. The rectory gardens (private) were designed by the famous, Le Notre, who often worked for Louis XIV and designed the famous gardens at Versaille. The church itself dates from the 13th century, though like many Berkshire churches was extensively restored in Victorian times. Within the church lies the mutilated effigy of Roger de Ingpen, the probable founder of the church. The effigy can be found on the northern side of the high alter, the traditional resting place for the church founder.*

As you leave the church, look for the sundial of 1649 and beneath it, the much earlier scratch dial.

The lane soon bends left and leads uphill where shortly after passing some large iron entrance gates on your right, you should look out for a stile and signposted public footpath on your left. Go over the stile beside a metal farm gate and continue for a few paces to pass through a second farm gate. Thereafter, you should carry straight on along a well defined track and continue to meet and cross a stile beside another metal gate. Immediately after, you will arrive at a small lane.

Turn left along the lane passing a thatched cottage on your right and at a junction turn right in the direction of the sign to Kintbury and Hungerford. If you are in need of refreshment it is a short detour from here to "The Swan Inn", free house, a popular local and one that not only serves real ale but specialises in Singaporean cuisine. To get there, continue for a few paces along the lane and fork left at the green. The inn is just a few metres along the lane on the right. You will need to retrace your steps to rejoin our route.

Returning to our route, continue for a few paces and then turn sharp right to follow a signposted footpath up a drive belonging to "Ingebrook House". As you reach the house, follow the path as it bends left away from the drive to run between hedgerows and thereafter, left behind a garden on your left. The footpath then bends sharply right to continue away from the houses along the left hand perimeter of a small field. Ahead of you in the distance now, is "Manor Farm", our next destination.

Follow the narrow winding footpath to soon cross a brook via a wooden bridge. Thereafter, follow the footpath through an area of brambles and cross two stiles to meet a grass track. Turn right along the grass track which runs gently uphill towards "Manor Farm". Just before the farm, turn left and pass through a metal gate signposted as a public footpath and follow a muddy track around the farm perimeter. Go over a stile beside a metal gate to meet a narrow lane which runs through the farm yard. Look out for the magnificent Georgian farmhouse at the southern end.

Turn left along the lane passing more farm buildings on your right and as the lane bends left, you should leave it to turn right over a stile onto a signposted footpath. This takes you into a field where you should continue straight across the field in the direction of the public footpath sign, heading for a chalet type bungalow in the distance. As you near the far end of the field, look out for a stile on your left beside an oak tree. Cross this into the next field which is also the grounds of a house with a wooden extension, ahead to your left. Continue straight on following the right hand perimeter and skirt to the right of a large laurel bush to meet a stile in the fence ahead.

Cross the stile to meet a driveway where you should turn left, following the driveway itself, which soons becomes concrete. Pass some stables on your right and continue ahead, where the concrete ends and the drive now becomes a grass track. Follow the track gently uphill to shortly meet a "T" junction, where you should turn right onto a prominent path which leads through a wood. You should ignore any minor turnings off and stay on the path which is at first lined by beech trees, a good guide to ensure you have taken the correct route.

Sometime on, ignore a crossing path to continue ahead between fields and eventually meet a lane. Cross the lane, pass through a gap in the fencing beside a metal gate and join a track ahead, signposted as a public footpath. The track runs in a straight line and passes through woodland, predominantly pine. As you continue you will pass over two small streams, the second via a wooden footbridge. You should stay on the footpath ignoring all turnings off to eventually meet a crossing path where there is a small stone on your right and a post with a number of footpath signs on your left.

Go over the crossing path carrying straight on and ignore a track off to your right marked as a bridleway. Pass to the left of the newly built "Inkpen Cottage" and continue to meet a lane where you will immediately see "The Crown and Garter" pub **(OS. 378639)**, a free house offering food and a pub garden full of animals - lop eared rabbits, cockerels, chickens, peacocks and a goat. The pub makes for an interesting stop.

Inkpen. *The pub roughly marks the centre of Inkpen. If you can remember, we entered Inkpen just before visiting the church. The rest of the village is much the same, houses scattered between fields and woodland with no apparent centre to unite them. The probable original centre was the church and rectory as there are some unusual earthworks there. These could be the remains of Inga's stockade. Inga was a Saxon chieftain and it is from him that Inkpen takes its name. Pen is an ancient word still used today, to describe a small enclosure or stockade.*

Apart from wood mills, Inkpen was once famous for its potteries which turned out, in the main, large hard wearing pots designed for constant use and not as ornaments. The local yellow clay used earned the potters of Inkpen the nickname of "Yellow

Legs". Today, there is still light industry in Inkpen as well as a large Morris Minor garage preserving the past in its own individual way.

Cross the lane and follow a track the other side which runs to the left of the pub and its car park. To your left at this point, the other side of a field on your left, is Inkpen Common which has a number of rare species of flora and forna. You will shortly meet a signposted bridleway on the left which offers a short detour to the common should you wish to pay a visit. You will however, have to retrace your steps to rejoin our route. There is also a signposted footpath on the right here which you should ignore.

Our route is straight on still following the track, to soon pass a beautiful brick cottage on your left, "Prossers Farm" and then cross a shallow valley with lovely views right to "Kirby House". At the far side of valley, pass a number of brick houses on the left and continue through an avenue of scotch pines to meet a lane. The wall ahead marks the perimeter of the historic "West Woodhay House", just visible.

Turn left along the lane and follow it as it bends right passing some of the outbuildings of "West Woodhay House", once the manor's farm. Pass a small green with a postbox bordered by low cut yews and continue straight on in the direction of the signs for West Woodhay Church, East Woodhay and Newbury. Pass the very grand gates to the house, opposite which is the old walled kitchen garden. Here through the gates, you can catch a glimpse of the grounds to the house, complete with picturesque lake.

West Woodhay House (OS. 385633 Map 174) *was designed and built by Inigo Jones in the early 17th century for the poet and politician, Sir Benjamin Rudyard. Inigo's reputation is upheld in this magnificent property which sits elegantly in beautifully landscaped grounds. Sir Benjamin must have found this a welcome refuge during his twentyfour turbulant years in Parliament. Being a man of sound morals, he frequently clashed with the authorities and did everything he could to avoid the Civil War. When there was no alternative, he sided with Hampden against King Charles, believing that this was the side of justice. He still worked for peace and urged "If the King draw one way, the Parliament another, we must all sink". In his constant efforts for peace he was eventually expelled from Parliament and he retired to West Woodhay, where he later died in May, 1658 at the grand age of eightysix.*

i

Stay on the lane which runs between white posts with the lake just mentioned on your right and soon after, look out for a signposted footpath on your left across a field, which you should take. Follow the right hand perimeter of the field heading for the spire of West Woodhay church in the distance. Take time however, as you cross the field to look back and enjoy the best view yet to "West Woodhay House". On meeting the church yard perimeter follow this round to meet and cross a stile, where you should continue to walk behind the church. As the church yard perimeter ends do not turn right, but continue straight on to go across a field. Looking back at this point will this time afford a picturesque view of the church, particularly attractive from this angle.

✝

The way across the field is somewhat undefined. You should therefore, head for a house with a metal gate in front of it at the far side. On reaching the metal gate go through this and turn right along a lane. After a short distance, at a junction, turn left. If however, you wish to visit West Woodhay church, then continue ahead at the junction for approxmately two hundred metres - you will need to retrace your steps to rejoin our route.

i
†

The Church of St. Laurence (OS. 391631 Map 174) *is the third church to occupy this site. The current church was built in 1883 and unusually, the only obvious relics of the previous churches are some attractive patterned tiles in the bell tower. Remembered here is General Sir Howard Elphinstone, who was awarded the VC in the Crimean War. In the grave yard, there is a small but beautiful garden created by Mr. J. Henderson in memory of his wife who was killed in a tragic riding accident.*

Turn left at the junction as mentioned, signposted to Faccombe and continue to pass yet another large house, "The Old Rectory", on the left. Just after, the lane bends left and you should leave it to turn right onto a concrete drive, signposted as a public bridleway and to "Highwood Farm". The bridleway runs along the right hand perimeter of a field with the farm itself directly ahead in the distance. Follow the bridleway and as the drive bends left to arrive at the farmhouse, you should leave it to continue straight on along a prominent farm track signposted as a public bridleway. You should ignore a signposted footpath off to the right here and shortly after, two tracks on your left which lead into the farm.

Stay on the track which soon runs across the centre of a field and after approximately one hundred metres, follow it as it bends left to approach the base of West Woodhay Down. It is now, you realise, that the easy walking is nearly over and that those calf muscles are about to be tested! The track leaves the field via a gap in the hedge and meets a lane. Cross the lane and follow a track the other side, signposted as a public bridleway. Make sure here, that you follow the track directly ahead which runs between banks and not one slightly to your left which is used by four wheel drive vehicles and can be extremely deep and muddy.

Follow the track between banks as it climbs West Woodhay Down, where the going can become very overgrown. If this is the case, you can climb the bank on your left and follow the four wheel drive track if the going is easier (hopefully at this point, you will have bypassed the worst of the mud!). As you progress, you will enjoy increasingly good views across the Kennet valley. The track you are following now acts as the border between Hampshire and Berkshire. The view nearer the top therefore, to the immediate left is Hampshire and to your right, Berkshire.

† At the top of the hill you will meet a "T" junction, a wide track which follows the ridge of the hill, the North Hants Ridgeway and now, also part of the Wayfarers Walk. Should you wish to shorten the walk, then turn right here and follow the track and then a lane back across Walbury Hill to reach our starting point. Our route and the main walk however, is left along the track which still acts as the border between Hampshire and Berkshire.

After some distance, pass a fenced area on the left now given over to natural habitation. Thereafter, pass a field on the left and look out for a farm gate, the entrance to the field **(OS. 392608)**. Do not go through this but turn right instead along an unmarked footpath, more a grass track, to go downhill. As a guide, the two aerial masts at the top of Combe Hill should be directly ahead of

The Church at West Woodhay

you. The footpath leads steeply downhill, bending gently right to descend into a valley. You should ignore an entrance to a field on your right and continue along the right hand perimeter of a field at the other side of the valley.

At the far side of the field the path leads up a small bank to reach a "T" junction in the form of a more prominent track. Turn right along the track which runs gently uphill between banks, lined in spring with a mass of snowdrops, and stay on the track as it bends left and then right. You will eventually meet a lane onto which you should turn left, heading for the aerial masts at the top of Combe Hill. Pass to the right of the aerial masts at the top of the hill (287m) and follow the lane enjoying the marvellous views over the surrounding countryside.

Shortly after the aerial masts the lane bends left and you should leave it here to continue ahead along a track, ignoring a signposted footpath off to your right. The track runs between fields and shortly follows woodland on the right. Thereafter, it continues once more between fields with lovely views to your right over a very steep valley known as Hogs Hole. It then enters woodland and it is here that we enter Hampshire for a short while.

As the woodland ends, ignore a track off to your right and continue straight on. At the other side of the valley now, is Combe Wood through which we will pass later on the walk. Also ahead to your right, is Hart Hill Down. The track leads downhill to eventually meet a lane at a "T" junction. Cross the lane and follow a lane ahead, signposted to Linkenholt and Andover and after approximately fifty metres, turn right onto a track signposted as a bridleway. You now have good views right of Walbury Hill.

The bridleway winds along the bottom of a picturesque shallow valley where after half a mile, you will pass an old brick and flint building on the left. In spring the area surrounding the building is covered with snowdrops and wild daffodils. A track leads off to the left at this point just after the outbuilding. This takes you to Linkenholt village, a total detour of one mile, but well worth a visit if you have time. Our route however, remains on the bridleway still along the valley bottom, this stretch of the route also being part of the Test Way. The large fields hereabouts are home to many hares, so keep your eyes peeled. (For more information on hares, see "The Hungerford Hare").

Sometime later, ignore a track off to the right and continue to pass a small brick barn on the right, after which the track bends round to the left. You will now be following the line of Hart Hill Down along the edge of Combe Wood. The track later enters a more wooded area and here you should ignore a track off to the right, which leads uphill through the wood. Look out also for a shepherd's caravan opposite (which I spotted at the time of writing) - a rare sight these days. You should also ignore a second track off to the right which is marked by a "no entry" sign. Further on, as the woodland on your right ends, you will arrive at a crossroads **(OS. 354595)** where you should take a track right leading along the perimeter of the wood.

Shortly after joining the track, ignore another track off to the left and carry straight on. Follow the track through the centre of Combe Wood ignoring all other tracks and turnings off. Your route is a long gradual climb and follows the spur of the wood which juts out into fields. The first sign you have of leaving the wood is a field on your left, albeit the wood continues for some distance on your right, gradually thinning down to nothing more than a hedgerow. Sometime later, you will meet a bridleway on your left which leads across a field to the Test Way. You should ignore this and continue straight on along the track, now signposted as a byway.

You will soon arrive at a crossing track which you should go straight over to continue ahead, now following a footpath the other side, a grass path bordered by hedges which leads over the top of Wadsmere Down (267 m). Continue over the crest of the down where there are clear views ahead of Walbury Hill fort and West Woodhay Down. Follow the footpath to descend the down steeply and soon enter woodland. As with many of the areas on this walk, the woodland floor here in spring is a mass of snowdrops and bluebells.

The track leaves the woodland where the views are once again quite spectacular. Nestling in the valley below is "Wrights Farm" and just beyond, the hamlet of Combe with its beautiful manor house and 12th century church. Stay on the track, still going downhill between banks to arrive at a small parking area which serves St. Swithun's church just passed on your left.

Combe Church and Manor (OS. 368607 Map 174) *are in a wonderful setting some distance from the hamlet they serve. The church is mainly 12th century with a few recent editions. The magnificent manor house is said to have played host to Charles II on his way to Marlborough.*

From the parking area, take the lane which forks left away from the church. There is a footpath here which runs along the right hand bank of the lane and may be safer to follow. On nearing the valley bottom however, you will have to leave the footpath and rejoin the lane to enter the pretty hamlet of Combe. As you enter, notice an old ornate wooden door on your right which is set into a wall.

On reaching the hamlet centre where Walbury Hill rises directly ahead of you, look out for a turning right signposted to "Lower Farm". Take this and pass "Boyd Cottage" on your left and thereafter, a lovely thatched cottage on your right. You should ignore a turning right to continue ahead and eventually pass "Lower Farm" itself. Stay on the track signposted as a byway, flanked by Walbury Hill on your left and Combe Hill on the right - offering no escape! As you progress, you can appreciate the security this area offered to the iron age people who built their hill fort here.

A Garden Door - Combe

Follow the track to begin your ascent of Walbury Hill where sometime later, the track bends right. You should leave it here and turn left onto a signposted public bridleway, a narrow path leading directly uphill. Further uphill, the path forks and you should take the left hand fork to continue your climb along a path which runs between steep banks. The path initially bears left up the side of the hill and then winds upwards between banks to reach the top.

After a short distance, you will arrive at open hillside. The views here are quite stunning and provide a good excuse for a rest. You should continue uphill along the path until you meet a crossing track. Turn right and follow the track still climbing to eventually arrive at a footpath sign beside a gate. Pass through the gate onto a track beside a lane and parking area. Turn left along the track, our old friend the North Hants Ridgeway, where shortly after a line of beech trees on your left will escort you between the ramparts of Walbury Hill fort.

Walbury Hill Fort, 297m/975ft, (OS. 375617 Map 174) *occupies the crown of Walbury Hill, the highest hill in Berkshire and the highest chalk hill in England. Needless to say, it is the highest point on our walk, so you can now relax. At 975ft, Walbury Hill is only 25ft short of the English definition of a mountain (1000ft) and consequently, commands unrivalled views over the local countryside.*

It is immediately obvious why the Celts built their fort here. Apart from the North Hants Ridgeway, there is no easy access to the fort and any enemies would have had to have been well prepared to even contemplate an attack. The fort was probably built during the early stages of the Iron Age around 500BC. It is at the western tip of a long line of forts which guard the North Hampshire Ridge. From its lofty height, many other forts are visible to the trained eye and on a clear day you can even see the hill fort on St. Catherine's Hill, near Winchester.

Walbury fort is especially large covering eightytwo acres and therefore, would have been very important in its day. Its earthen banks would have been strengthened by a timber rampart and judging by the size of the fort, it would have protected a population of approximately one thousand.

The Celts were a tribal people and very war like. More often than not, battles were between rival forts or tribes rather than with a common enemy. The favourite weapon was the sling, which proved useful in repelling attacks. For close combat the warriors were armed with knives, swords and shields for protection. Amongst the prized spoils of war, were their opponents heads which would be hacked from the bodies of their victims and then errected on poles around the fort. The heads of more important victims were preserved in cedar oil and kept at the chieftain's house to be shown off to visitors.

If Walbury has aroused your interest in Celtic life, then I recommend a visit to the Museum of the Iron Age at Andover (Tel: 0264 66283).

Carry straight on across the centre of the fort where the views are worth stopping for, many being instantly familiar, having been part of our walk today. As you continue, the gibbet passed at the beginning of the walk also comes into view. Carry straight on to pass through the ramparts at the other side of the hill fort and return to the car park which was our starting point.

ACCOMMODATION

The Jack Russell, Faccombe. Tel: 026487 315
One and a quarter miles from the walk, this is a very local pub with its very own atmosphere and one that makes you feel immediately welcome. The owners take great pride in their work which is reflected in the accommodation. A CAMRA - North Hampshire pub of the summer in 1990!

Beacon House, Upper Inkpen/Green. Tel: 0488 668640
One mile from the walk, this is a wonderful place to stay with your accommodation in the shadow of Walbury Hill, which is such a feature on the walk. If you enjoy peaceful rural surroundings, then this is for you.

Youth Hostel.
The nearest youth hostel that I intended to recommend, has unfortunately just closed down (Overton). Accordingly, the only other I can offer, but not that close, is Court Hill Ridgeway Centre (Tel: 02357 60253). For more details, see Accommodation under "The Downland Dare".

Camping and Caravanning, Oakley Farm Caravan Park, Washwater. Tel: 0635 36581
Twelve and a half miles from the walk, this is an attractive site close to the outskirts of Newbury.

THE LAMBOURN LUNGE

Distance: 14⅛ miles (22.65 km)
Time: Allow approximately 7 hours
Map: Ordnance Survey Landranger Map 174

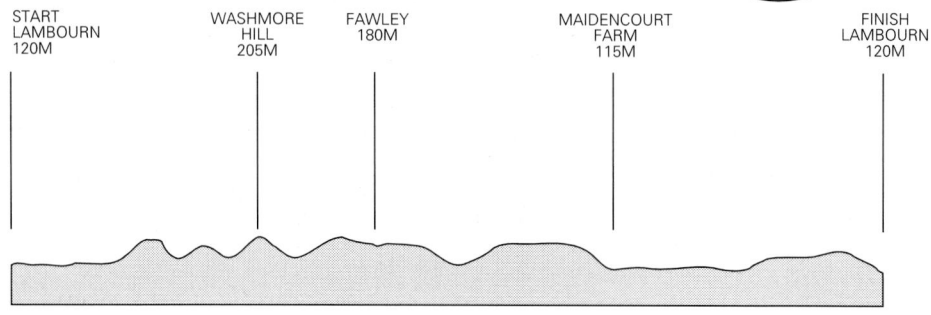

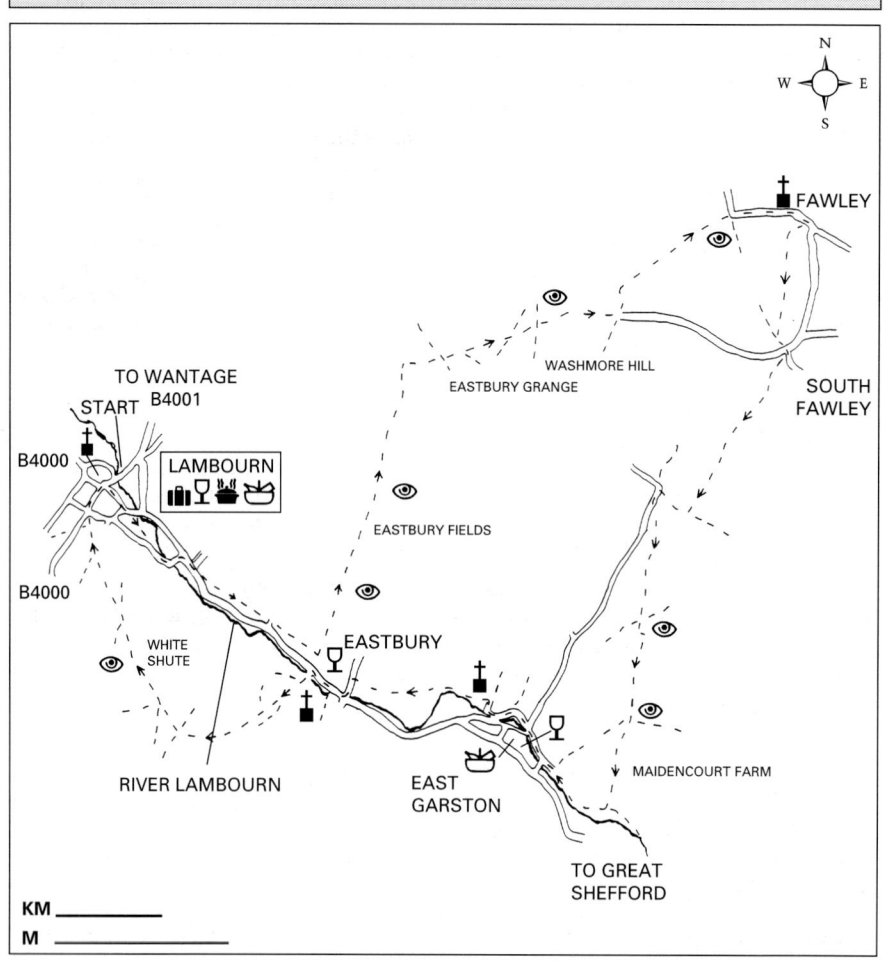

THE LAMBOURN LUNGE
BERKSHIRE

START	WASHMORE	FAWLEY	MAIDENCOURT	FINISH
LAMBOURN	HILL	180M	FARM	LAMBOURN
120M	205M		115M	120M

90

Walk Summary

A horse lover would immediately tell you that any walk around Lambourn will feature more horses than walkers. For as the town sign informs you, Lambourn is the valley of the race horse. The wild grass covered Lambourn Downs make an ideal training ground for race horses and I can guarantee you will see more than one horse on the walk. The majority of the walk takes you over the downs, past lonely farms and through forgotten villages, before descending into the relatively tame Lambourn valley. Here you follow the river Lambourn upstream passing through the sleepy villages of East Garston and Eastbury, before making a brief excursion onto the downs once more to reach Lambourn.

The difference in terrain between the downs and the valley means a walk of two different characters. The downs can be wild and bleak, especially in winter, whereas the sheltered valley has the gentle hint of summer throughout the year. Some of the tracks are frequently used by horses and can become extremely muddy, so make sure you wear those boots. If you are worried about the title of this walk, don't - the "lunge" is not what you are expected to do en route, it is the term for a long rope used to train horses.

Start - OS. 326789 Map 174

The walk starts at the centre of Lambourn in front of the church. To get there, if coming via the M4, leave it at junction 14 and at the roundabout take the northern exit signposted to Wantage. After a short distance, turn left onto the B4000 and follow it to reach Lambourn. Take care though, as the B4000 is not a continuous road and at one point you will need to take a turning right, opposite "The Swan". If coming from Wantage, you are better off leaving Wantage via the B4507 and then turning south onto the B4001. The B4001 takes you all the way to Lambourn. The beauty of this route is that it takes you over the Lambourn Downs, giving you a taste of what is to come - that is, if it doesn't scare you off! If coming from Hungerford, the best and most picturesque route is via the B4192 and at Chilton Foliat, turn right onto the B4001. Follow the road and pass under the M4 to meet the B4000 which leads you into Lambourn.

There is no obvious alternative start. The nearest train station is at Hungerford, from where there are regular bus services to Lambourn.

THE LAMBOURN LUNGE

Before we brave the Lambourn Downs, it is worth discovering the town from where we start.

Lambourn (OS. 326789 Map 174) *is the capital of the Lambourn valley. The tower of its proud Norman church rises above the town to act as a landmark for miles around. Man was living hereabouts several centuries before the Normans came and built their church. To the north of the town are a number of burial mounds, built by men who worked the downs with tools of flint.*

Later, it is claimed, the most respected of all Saxon kings, Alfred the Great, was born here. What is certain, is that Alfred had a palace here and land which he left to his wife, Eahlswitha. The site of the palace is uncertain, though it is believed it is where the powerful medieval family, the Essex's, later built their palace. Unfortunately, this too has also disappeared.

In the middle ages, Lambourn was granted a market and two fairs. Lambourn then became Chipping Lambourn, "chipping" being an old word for a market, usually one selling sheep. The name Lambourn is probably derived from two words, "Lamb" relating to sheep, which have long been farmed on the surrounding downs, and "bourne", an old word for an intermittent stream. "Bourne" describes the Lambourn river perfectly, as it is well known to dry up at certain times of the year.

The old market cross, erected when the town was granted its market, still stands in front of the church. Sheep were the principal industry of the town until the 18th century when the Earls of Craven (see The Water Chase), started horse racing at their newly built house, "Ashdown Park" (N.T.). It was quickly recognised that the surrounding downs were ideal for training horses and the town's importance as a race horse centre grew steadily. The town now lives for horse racing, all around there are stables and training gallops. Horse owners, trainers and jockeys fill the streets and much of the local industry is based around horse racing, from the construction of horse boxes to a corner shop selling riding gear. Even the lynch gate to the church is in memory of a Victorian race horse owner, William Jousiffe.

With the race meets at Newbury, the whole town appears to move house and if you have any ideas of getting anywhere in a hurry, forget it. Lambourn must, in fact, be one of the few places in England where the horse has stood up to the motor car. The large number of horses on the roads around the town have forced the council to create special horse tracks to enable horses and riders to reach the open hills without having to use roads. If you are genuinely interested in horses, then by special arrangement the Lambourn Trainers Association will give you a guided tour. The tour which takes approximately two hours, takes you around the stables and gallops and allows you to meet some of the horses. To make an appointment, tel. 0488 72664.

Horses apart, Lambourn has some respectable literary associations. Charles Kingsley wrote fondly of Lambourn and Thomas Hardy less so. Joshua Silvester, a well known 17th century poet, found inspiration from the valley and money from Sir William Essex, who became his patron.

The church is well worth a look round, it has an interesting 14th century window and some well preserved brasses. There is also a magnificent alabaster tomb of Sir Thomas Essex. In the church yard, there is a gravestone remembering John Carter, who was hanged for trying to set fire to the town. He is one of several claimants to be the last man hanged for arson in England. North of the church lies the most picturesque part of the village. Here cobbles can still be found as well as some old alm houses, built in 1502. For refreshments, Lambourn has several small shops and of the more warming kind, there is "The George Hotel", Arkells Ales, "The Red Lion", Charrington and my favourite, "The Wheelrights Arms", Morlands. All three establishments offer food.

Wisely deciding to try the pubs at the end of the walk, take the lane opposite the church, Newbury Street, between "The George" and "The Red Lion" and pass a racing and hunting saddlers shop on your right. Follow the lane which passes a mixture of pretty Georgian houses and picturesque cottages and ignore any turnings off, looking out for a chip shop on the right. Just after this, take a signposted footpath right, part of the Lambourn Valley Way, also signposted as Blind Lane. The Lambourn Valley Way incidentally, is a twenty-two mile linear walk from Uffington White Horse to Newbury and follows the Lambourn valley. After approximately twenty metres, ignore a path off to the right to continue straight on, still following the signs for the Lambourn Valley Way. A few paces on, go over a crossing path to continue ahead through a small modern housing estate and at the other side pass through a kissing gate onto some playing fields.

Go straight across the playing fields in the direction of the yellow arrows of the Lambourn Valley Way and after a short distance, pass to the left of a club house to continue ahead through the car park. At the far side, go over a stile into a field and follow the right hand perimeter ahead to meet and cross another stile onto a lane. Bear left along the lane and follow it as it bends left over a bridge across the river Lambourn. Thereafter, follow the lane to arrive at a "T" junction where you should turn right along a road, signposted to Shefford and Newbury.

After approximately fifty metres and after the last house on the left, turn left onto a lane signposted to Longhedge. Immediately upon joining the lane, turn right up a small bank into a field, in the direction of the Lambourn Valley Way sign and continue along the right hand perimeter of the field which runs parallel to the road on the right and in the distance on the same side, the Lambourn river.

After a short distance the field perimeter bends left. Our route however, is straight on passing over a stile into the next field. Again you should follow the right hand field perimeter, where the footpath is now slightly above the road and affords excellent views right across to "Bockhampton Manor Stables". The name "Bockhampton" is all that remains of a medieval village which once stood on this site.

Go straight across the field and approximately two thirds of the way across, look out for a small gate and fence on your right. Pass through the gate and turn immediately left to follow the left hand perimeter of the next field. At the end of the field, cross two stiles into another field, now much larger and continue ahead going straight across the field to meet and cross another stile in some bushes. Carry straight on through a small line of bushes and pass through a kissing gate into the next field.

Go straight across the centre of the field and cross a stile at the far side. Go over a track and then a stile to reach a field the other side. Again, you should go straight across the field, still signposted as part of the Lambourn Valley Way. The first buildings of Eastbury village should now be in view ahead to your right. After a short distance, the path will follow the right hand field perimeter passing behind some houses. It then runs beside a line of bungalows to meet a metal gate. Do not pass through the gate but turn left immediately before it, and continue for approximately twenty paces before turning right onto a signposted footpath. This runs between fields heading for a barn ahead.

Pass to the right of the barn to meet a track onto which you should turn left and go uphill away from Eastbury to climb what is known as Eastbury Fields. You are now leaving the Lambourn Valley Way and the relative ease of the valley to tackle the more strenuous Lambourn Downs. The base for the hedgerows which border the track is wild rose, offering a mass of colour and heady scent in summer and a vital source of food for birds in winter. As you continue, you will enjoy superb views back over the Lambourn valley.

At the top of Eastbury Fields (200m), the track levels out and the hedgerows give way to open views over the Lambourn Downs and north to the Ridgeway, an ancient track running along the crest of the downs (see The Downland Dare). The track continues to cross the plateau of Eastbury Fields before descending, becoming steeper as you go, into a remote valley. At the valley bottom cross over a wide grass track used for race horse training and continue straight up the other side of the valley, the climb being much gentler than your recent descent. Ignore a track off to the right and continue ahead, where the track you are following is now more prominent and well used by horses. To your right now are good views of Washmore Hill, identifiable by its lonely larch which stands at the summit.

After a short distance, pass a track off to the left and continue straight on to the top of the valley side and pass a small strip of woodland, again on the left. Immediately after, ignore another track on the left and continue to cross a wide grass track, part of the same training route for race horses crossed earlier. Soon after, go over a second crossing track and carry straight on following a line of scots pines on the right. At the end of the pines, the track bears gently left and continues downhill passing a newly planted area of woodland. You will soon meet a "T" junction where you should turn right to follow a wide track, running parallel with a line of telegraph poles along a shallow valley.

After a short distance, the telegraph poles bear right away from the track to service a house just visible, "Eastbury Grange". Do not follow the telegraph poles, but continue along the track to eventually meet a junction of tracks beside a farm yard. You should ignore all turnings off and carry straight on along the track, passing to the left of the farm yard. You will probably have realised by now, that this part of the walk can be extremely muddy in wet weather. Soon after the farm yard, you should ignore another track off to the right signposted as a byway and continue your route ahead.

Approximately fifty paces on, the track forks. You must take the left hand track to climb the side of Washmore Hill with good views to your left of "Warren Farm". The track continues uphill to the summit (205m high), the second highest point on the walk **(OS. 368804)**.

The Downs. *From here there are panoramic views over the downs, the scenery is wild and simple. There are no hidden corners, just exposed rolling hills which can be frightening or beautiful depending on the weather. The thing I like about this area are the down to earth names given to the land by the people who have lived here over the centuries. There are no traces of obscure legend, but simple descriptive names which at once have a meaning for the stranger. For example, surrounding us with reference to the rabbits that live hereabouts, "Warren Down", "Warren Plantation", "Old Warren Wood" and two "Warren" farms. With reference to sheep, there is "Ewe Hill" and "Sheep Drove". Some more names with obvious connections are "Crow Down", "Wormhill", "Cranes Copse", "Cockcrow Bottom" and perhaps most interestingly of all, "Poacher's Folly". One thing that has always puzzled me though, is the origin of the name of the hill on which we are standing, Washmore Hill.*

At the top of Washmore Hill, there is a larch tree and two tracks, one leading left and the other right. You should ignore both tracks to continue straight on along a much more prominent track, which can be very muddy in winter and wet conditions. The track soon begins to descend with views ahead of "Old Warren Farm", our next destination, and after half a mile meets a small tarmac lane on a bend. Turn left here onto the lane following the sign to "Old Warren" and "Littleworth", also marked as a private road.

Follow the lane as it bends left and then right to skirt "Old Warren" farmhouse. Until recently, this old farmhouse relied upon a three hundred foot well for water.

There is a remarkable story of a Victorian lady who fell into the well, being saved only by the hoops in her dress which wedged in the well sides. As the lane bends left again, leave it turning right for approximately thirty paces to reach a wooden gate. Do not pass through the gate, but turn left immediately before it to follow a grass footpath which runs between fences. This runs gently downhill passing woodland on your right and at the bottom runs into a field, where you should follow the left hand perimeter passing an unusual footpath sign to once again go uphill. Pass another strip of woodland on the left and follow the field perimeter as it bends, to commence another ascent adjacent to more woodland with a mass of rabbit warrens.

At the left hand corner of the field, turn right to continue along the field perimeter to reach a footpath sign. Turn left here before the field perimeter bends left, to enter another field. Do not turn left, but continue straight on along a grass track which follows the right hand perimeter of the field. At the far side, pass through a metal gate and continue on the track which follows the left hand perimeter of the next field. At the end of the field, the track meets a lane where on your right there is a bridleway and a trig point which indicates that you are now 206 metres above sea level.

Congratulations! You are now at the highest point on the walk. From here there are more good views and it is possible to pick out two of the most prominent hill forts in the area. To the south east, Beacon Hill, which is situated on the north Hampshire Ridge above Highclere and to the north west, Uffington, home to the White Horse and famous in legend. To the north a lane leads to the Ridgeway and another famous hill fort, although not visible, Segsbury.

Ignore the bridleway right and carry straight on along the lane heading for Fawley, our next destination. A line of beech trees topped by noisy circling rooks, is the first sign that you are entering Fawley proper, where in spring the base of the trees are a mass of snowdrops. Continue to pass the old village school on your right and look out for the church ahead which should now be in view. Welcome to Fawley.

The Church as you approach Fawley

Fawley (OS. 391814 Map 174) *is most famous for its Hardy connection. It is almost certain that Mary Hardy, Thomas Hardy's grandmother, was born at Fawley. She was an orphan and remembers an unhappy upbringing in the village. Thomas Hardy curious to try and trace any relations in the village, persuaded his sister to visit. She came in 1864 and liked what she saw, though no trace of their relations could she find, nor anyone who could remember their grandmother. A year or two later, Hardy himself visited the village. Unlike his sister, he found Fawley a gloomy place and described a nearby valley as "the valley of brown melancholy".*

Later Hardy used Fawley in his tragic novel, "Jude the Obscure". In the book, he called Fawley "Marygreen" and used the village as the starting place for Jude's unfortunate life. Many of the features of the village are still recognisable from the book, most prominent are the noisy rooks which Jude was paid to keep off a farmer's field. The school, now a private house, still stands and the pretty thatched cottage which was the village bakery and where Jude lived with his fearful aunt Drusilla, still exists opposite the church, though the bakery frontage has now gone.

The most distinctive building in the village is the church. This replaced a medieval church in 1866. It was designed by George Edmund Street who was one of the leading Victorian architects of his day and greatly influenced by his travels in Europe. Hardy was not impressed by the church and commented on Street as, "A certain obliterator of historic records who had run down from London and back in a day". The building of the new church was funded by Blanch Wroughton who lived at "Woolley House". She saw the church as a memorial to her late husband and a gift to the village, of which she was effectively Lord of the Manor. There is a fine alabaster memorial tablet to Blanch Wroughton in the church. Another memorial records the death of her grandson, Phillip, who was killed in Palestine in 1917. A huge granite cross at the side of the A338 Hungerford to Wantage road, also remembers his tragic end.

Despite its literary connections, Fawley remains a remote and unpretentious village, beautiful in its simple honest appearance. Gloomy it certainly is not, though you can make up your own mind.

Follow the road through Fawley which bends around the church and pass a thatched cottage (the old bakery) on the right, after which you will meet a small green on the same side. Look out here for a signposted public footpath across the green which you should follow. After the green stay on the footpath, which bends right to pass behind the cottages and houses of the village. As it bends right again back to the road, leave it to take a very narrow path left which can at times be difficult to define. It does however become more prominent as you continue.

The path leads through scrubland which in spring is full of snowdrops and passes behind the remains of an ornamental garden on your right before entering a large field. Here you should follow the hedgerow which runs ahead of you for a short distance and thereafter, continue straight on across the centre of the field. The path can be somewhat undefined and you should maintain your line across the field to reach a ridge at the centre. From here, continue straight on across the field, heading for a hedgerow running south from the perimeter hedge of the field you are in. On reaching the far side, look out for a small gap in the hedgerow through which you should pass to reach the corner of another field. Continue ahead along the left hand perimeter following the hedgerow running south.

Suddenly, the hedgerow gives way and South Fawley, our next destination, comes into view ahead. On reaching the edge of the village, you will meet a track coming in from the right which runs through a farm yard to reach the heart of South Fawley, predominantly a farming based community. Turn left onto the track and follow it through the farm yard. The track leads out to the village centre, made up of the farm and a few cottages which surround a muddy pool, all that is left of the village pond. Continue to reach a "T" junction at a lane (as a guide, there is a Post Box and road sign here on your right). Cross the lane and follow another lane ahead, where to the left you will catch glimpses of the castle-like "Fawley Manor".

i **Fawley Manor (OS. 391801 Map 174)** *is a magnificent Jacobean manor house* built in 1614 by Sir Francis Moore, reputed to have been a distant relative of the famous martyr, Sir Thomas Moore. The Moore's were devout Catholics and the tower which you can just see, used to house the chapel. Being Catholics, the Moore's were loyal to the King and during the Civil War, the manor was used to house the King's lifeguards. This part of Berkshire saw more action than most during the war, two important battles being fought not far from here at Newbury. The Moore's now rest in the family vault in the old church yard at Fawley. During the rebuilding of the new church, the vault was opened and all the bodies were found in a state of perfect preservation. On the breast of Lady Francis lay a glass phial said to contain a secret potion. The vault was re-sealed and the Moore's left to rest in peace.

Follow the lane for a few paces until you meet a track on your right, signposted as a public footpath. Take this to leave South Fawley, passing between a house on the left and a number of cottages set back to your right, the latter now sadly derelict. Continue downhill between fields and on reaching the bottom of a valley, follow the track as it bends left and later right. Here you should ignore a grass track going straight on to continue your

Petrol pump in farmyard - South Fawley

route along the main track, which can be extremely muddy in wet or wintry weather. After a short distance the track begins a gradual climb uphill, initially following a wood on the left, Well Copse, and thereafter, open fields.

As you continue your climb, a large farm will come into view in the valley below to your left. Shortly after, you will pass a horse trodden track leading in a straight line down the side of the hill to the farm. The horse tracks are a clue that the farm is in fact "Whatcombe", one of a number of famous racing stables that take advantage of the springy turf of the downs.

Whatcombe (OS. 392789 Map 174) *is particularly well known in racing circles having trained many winners over the years. One of them, Blandford, is buried in the grounds. Whatcombe however, has not always been a stables. Centuries ago, it was a thriving village with its own manor house and so word has it, a monastery. The monastery is said to have had a secret passage to the manor at South Fawley, though years of searching have found nothing. The only clue left to the monastery is a small field which is still called Nuns Walk. The village church now forms part of the present house. Its bells it is said, were stolen and melted down to make the bells of East Garston church.*

The only trace of the old manor is a gloomy muddy pool, once part of the manor garden. Before dutch elm disease, three proud elms protected the pond, known as Adam, Eve and the Serpent. One tree died before the other two and the locals insisted that this was the Serpent.

Any curiosity to explore "Whatcombe" must be suppressed as the track to "Whatcombe" is private and our route is straight on. On reaching the top of Kite Hill, you will pass a narrow strip of woodland on the right where the track bends right to eventually meet a lane **(OS. 378789)**. Turn left along the lane where there are superb views over the Lambourn valley and after approximately fifty metres, leave the lane and turn left onto a signposted byway.

The byway immediately bends right and continues along the right hand perimeter of a field. Follow it and pass through a gap in the hedge where it bends left. Here you should leave the byway and continue straight on along a less defined track following the right hand field perimeter, which runs along the left hand side of a steep sided valley. After three quarters of a mile, you will meet a bridleway which to your right descends to the valley below and to the left runs across fields over Trindledown to "Northfield Farm". You should ignore this and carry straight on heading for a copse.

On reaching the copse the track bends left, contrary to the ordnance survey map route. You should follow the track around the copse, ignoring a track left as you continue. The copse narrows to a pleasant grass area which is a perfect place to rest and admire the views. Thereafter, stay on the track which follows a broad tree lined ridge with continuous excellent views east and west. It eventually arrives at a trig point **(186m - OS. 375769)**, where you should ignore a footpath off to the left and continue straight on along the track. You now start your descent into the Lambourn valley, the going becoming steeper as you progress. You should ignore a track right to continue ahead with the buildings of "Maidencourt Farm" now in view.

It is not long before you reach the farm and pass through a metal gate to go through the farm yard to the left of a large Georgian farmhouse. Look out for the unusual farm sign made up of farm tools. Carry straight on and follow the farm drive until you meet a bridge over the river Lambourn. Do not cross the bridge but turn right just before it and walk upstream along the right hand bank, where you are now back on the Lambourn Valley Way. Continue to pass through a garden, at the far side of which you should go through a kissing gate and carry straight on across a field with the Lambourn on your left.

At the far side of the field, pass through another kissing gate into the next field and maintain your route ahead. At the end of the field there is a small fenced area on your left entering the Lambourn itself, given over for horses to drink. Just after this, the field ends and you should pass through a kissing gate to meet a track. Continue straight on along the track to arrive at a lane with stables on your right. Bearing left here along the lane over the Lambourn would take you to "The Queens Arms Hotel", a smart free house. This pub is good for an after walk rest, but en route it is probably worth waiting for the more down to earth "Plough" at Eastbury, only a couple of miles further on.

Our route is ahead along the lane through East Garston, still signposted as the Lambourn Valley Way and bordered by picturesque cottages for which East Garston is famous.

East Garston (OS. 365768 Map 174) *is constantly featured in countryside journals and picture calendars and rightly so. For it is this type of village which has given rise to the expression "picture postcard". Through the centre of the village winds the river Lambourn, over which numerous wooden plank and more ornate bridges lead to inviting homesteads. The Lambourn Downs which overlook the village once harboured sheep farming, the proceeds of which enabled the villagers to build the much admired properties we see today. The name of the village is derived from a Saxon, Esgar, who was responsible for the horses of King Harold and owned the land* on which East Garston now stands. Esgar fought for the King at the Battle of Hastings and for his trouble was forced to hand over his land to the Normans.

Sheep farming in the area has now given way to horses, with two racing stables attached to the village. Apart from "The Queens Arms", the village has a general stores should you need to re-stock after your efforts on the downs.

Following the lane through the village, it is not long before you meet a bridge over the river the other side of which is a Post Office and general stores. Also on your right is a lane with a barn which displays a plaque confirming the village's inclusion in the Domesday Book. Directly behind the barn is an old railway bridge, the last remains of a railway line which used to serve the valley, sadly closed in 1959. Do not turn off here, but carry straight on walking parallel with the river Lambourn through the village. Pass a small chapel on your left, now converted into a private house and shortly after, pass another bridge over the river leading to a small green and war memorial. You should continue along the lane now signposted as a dead end.

After passing a line of beautiful thatched cottages follow the lane as it bends right to head for the church. Just before the lane becomes a track to enter a farm yard and the church entrance, you should leave it to turn left over a stile onto a fenced path signposted as the Lambourn Valley Way. If you wish to visit the church however, do not take the fenced path but take the drive left immediately after. You will need to retrace your steps to rejoin our route. The church (which every time I have tried to visit has been locked), dates back to Norman times. However, extensive restoration between 1876 and 1882 has all but wiped out any traces of that period.

Follow the Lambourn Valley Way to cross another stile onto what was once the Lambourn Valley railway line. Pass to the left of the church yard which in spring is carpeted with daffodils and stay on the railway line for approximately a quarter of a mile, at one point passing over a small bridge. Sometime after, the path reaches an abrupt end where you should ascend some steps on the left into a field. Turn right and follow the field perimeter, with views over Eastbury and beyond it, Cleeve Hill.

At the end of the field go over a muddy crossing track and carry straight on along a grass track, still part of the Lambourn Valley Way. As the track ends you should continue ahead following a narrow path along the right hand perimeter of a field. The path then enters Eastbury by running behind a garden, before descending some steep steps to meet a lane. Turn left along the lane to reach the main street at Eastbury, passing as you go a huge barn on your left and an octagonal dovecote on the right.

The Dovecote (OS. 348771 Map 174) *is a rare example of its type. The apertures through which the doves entered are now blocked up. When in use the doves could nest on nine hundred and ninety-nine purpose built chalk block platforms. An internal spiral staircase made egg collecting from these platforms easy. The dovecote was once in the grounds of "Pigeon House", (still part of the village today), which was owned by the Black Monks of Wallingford. The house was used as a retreat enabling the monks to rest from the rigours of daily life.*

On meeting the main road beside a bus stop, cross this and take a lane the other side which bears right to run through the centre of Eastbury. (Do not make the mistake of continuing ahead up the hill).

Eastbury (OS. 347772 Map 174), *like East Garston, is another village deserving of the term "picture postcard" and, as with its neighbour, the river Lambourn runs* *through its centre. It is quite common for the river to burst its banks and this explains the sandbags which are stored in neat piles around the village in readiness. At the centre of the village stands the old forge, with a selection of different styles of horse shoe adorning its door, each clearly labelled. A number of footbridges lead over the river, the one opposite the church you may notice is wider than the others. This was to accommodate a hand cart hearse.*

The church itself, dedicated to St. James the Greater, was built in 1853 by the Rector, Robert Millman, who went on to become the Bishop of Calcutta. It was designed by George Street, who as we now know, was also responsible for the church at Fawley. Usually, a church of this type attracts only a passing glance. This one though, has a feature which brings people from all over. In 1971, a finely engraved window was installed in the south wall. It was engraved by Laurence Whistler to celebrate the lives of the poet Edward Thomas and his wife Helen, who lived in the village during her final years. Her grave can be found at the top of the church yard beneath some young beech trees. The window is truly beautiful and depicts a landscape which subtly recalls the poet's life and writings. Amongst the grasses at the bottom of the window is hidden the date on which Edward Thomas was killed whilst in action near Arras, France.

Opposite the church on the other side of the river, stands the prayer cross of St. Antoline. Its steps were used by travelling preachers as a platform to pass on their messages to often mocking crowds. At the Lambourn end of the village stands a magnificent manor built by the powerful Fitzwarines. It is here that we also find "The Plough", a popular local free house with a welcome for the weary walker in the form of good ale and wholesome food.

After passing the old forge you should ignore a signposted footpath on the left to continue past the church and reach the lane end in front of the manor house and another property, signposted as "The Old Iron House". On your right is the welcome site of "The Plough".

Take the bridleway left beside "The Old Iron House", and follow it as it leads uphill affording lovely views back over Eastbury village and Eastbury Fields beyond. Ignore a turning left and another right just after the last house on the right and continue uphill for some distance until the bridleway forks. Take the right hand track which follows the base of the curved wooded slope to Cleeve Hill, which can be very muddy in wet weather. Stay on the track to eventually meet and go over a crossing track and follow a footpath the other side across a field.

At the far side of the field go over a stile onto a track where you should turn right to follow the track, a byway known locally as White Shute, once the old road between Lambourn and Hungerford. As you progress you will see a stile on your right which leads onto natural chalk downlands. These are The Watts, (White Shute) Nature Reserve, a site of special scientific interest, acquired in 1991. The downlands are open to the public and this is a lovely place for a rest before your final trek into Lambourn.

Continue along the track where on the left in the distance is a white cottage. This is "Bold Start Farm" and I have often wondered about its origin to have such a name. The track now leads uphill, a final test of your stamina, with views behind over Cleeve Hill and continues to take you over the top of Coppington Hill. Here, again, there are superb views over the Lambourn valley, with the church tower at Lambourn now visible, our next and final destination!

Follow the track downhill ignoring all turnings off to reach the outskirts of the village beside some stables on your left. After the latter, the track gently climbs, passing a number of houses on the left and some more stables on the right, "Meridian Stud". It then goes downhill gradually changing from a track into asphalt. You should ignore all turnings off and continue, passing to the left of a school. Shortly after, the track now a lane, bends right to continue downhill. You should leave it here to carry straight on, downhill between banks, along a signposted bridleway. This takes you to the village High Street, the B4000, onto which you should turn right. Follow the High Street and ignore all turnings off until you reach the centre of Lambourn and the church, which was our starting point.

If you have not already done so, booking into one of the welcoming hotels for a hot bath and a good night's rest is perhaps now the only sensible option.

ACCOMMODATION

The Red Lion, Lambourn. Tel: 0488 71406
The George, Lambourn. Tel: 0488 71889
Both hotels are on the walk. In competition with each other, there is little to choose between them. Both offer comfortable accommodation and are lively local pubs. The choice may not be which one you prefer but which has a room free.

Lodge Down, Lambourn. Tel: 0672 40304
Virtually on the walk, accommodation is in a large farmhouse with fine views over the Lambourn Downs. A comfortable residents lounge has a cosy open fire to warm you in winter.

Youth Hostel, The Court Hill Ridgeway Centre YHA. Tel: 02357 60253
Approximately four miles from the walk, this is a purpose built hostel from the reconstruction of four barns. The hostel is in a beautiful position with views over the Vale of the White Horse. The grounds include a wood where you can camp and has a barbecue area.

Camping & Caravanning, Oakley Farm Caravan Park, Washwater. Tel: 0635 36581
Approximately seventeen miles from the walk, this is an attractive site close to the outskirts of Newbury.

N.B. If you are a Camping & Caravan Club member, there is a superb site at Farncombe Farm, near Lambourn. Tel: 0488 71833. For membership details, Tel: 0203 69499

THE DOWNLAND DARE

Distance: 16¼ miles (25.25 km)
Time: Allow approximately 8½ hours
Map: Ordnance Survey Landranger Map 174

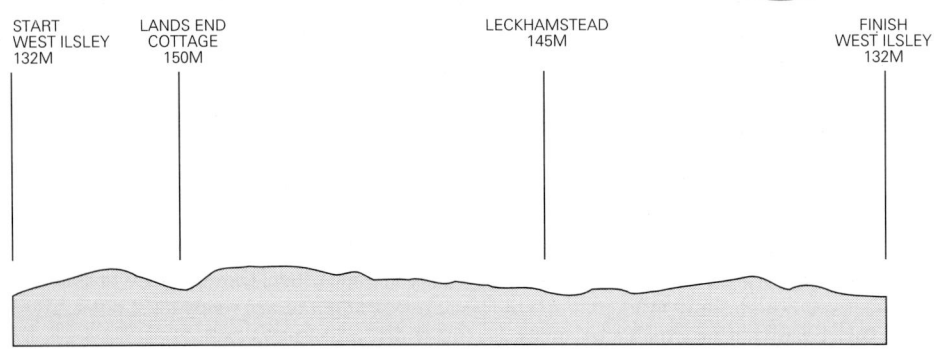

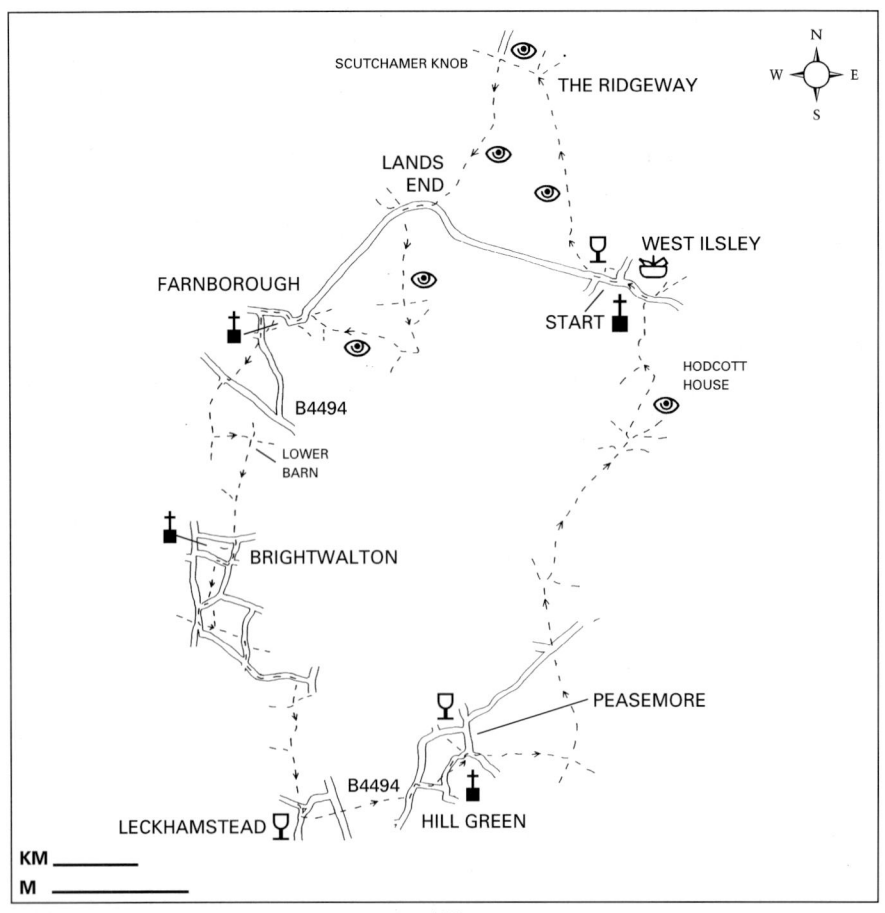

START	LANDS END	LECKHAMSTEAD	FINISH
WEST ILSLEY	COTTAGE	145M	WEST ILSLEY
132M	150M		132M

Walk Summary
This is the challenge walk of the book and if you dare to do it, one, make sure you are fit and two, ensure you pack plenty of provisions. The route explores the northern edge of the Lambourn Downs with the constant reward of superb views. Most of the walk crosses the open downland for which this area is famed, though this means you may be exposed to the elements. In summer this is the sun and heat and in winter, wind chill. The other factor to bear in mind, is that although there are no steep ascents, the route is certainly not level and as always when you are tired, there appears to be more "ups" than "downs". I hope all this has not put you off, for the walk more than compensates by taking you through some of the least explored areas of Berkshire. All I am trying to emphasise is go prepared.

Start - OS. 471826 Map 174
The walk starts at West Ilsley in front of "The Harrow", which is situated opposite the cricket green at the western end of the village. To get there, if coming from any direction south, make your way to junction 13 of the M4 which is the interchange with the A34, Newbury to Abingdon road. At the roundabout, head north following the signs for Oxford. After approximately five and a half miles, turn left onto a road signposted to East Ilsley, West Ilsley and Compton and almost immediately after, turn right in the direction of the sign to West Ilsley. Continue through the village until you meet "The Harrow". There is a small parking area in front of a pond here or if this is full, road side parking is possible. If coming from the north, join the A34 west of Didcot and head south towards Newbury. Just after a garage, leave the A34 to take a road signposted to West Ilsley and The Ridgeway. Turn right to go over the A34 and at a roundabout, continue straight on to follow a road over Bury Down into West Ilsley. Turn right, signposted to Farnborough and Wantage and continue until you reach "The Harrow".

Alternative starts can be made from any of the villages en route. The nearest railway stations are at Didcot or Newbury. At the time of writing, it is possible to get a bus from either town to West Ilsley.

THE DOWNLAND DARE

West Ilsley is a lovely village to explore and "The Harrow", an added attraction. In view of the length of our adventure however, it is best to leave these treats until the end.

To start, from the parking area, walk away from the village passing "The Harrow" pub on your right and the cricket pitch on your left. Shortly after the pub, turn right onto a track signposted as a bridleway. The bridleway passes between pretty cottages before continuing between fields, heading for the Ridgeway.

After some distance, the track divides into three. The track on the left is grass and on the far right, chalk. Our route however, is along the track in the middle which soon bends right in front of a gate. It then climbs quite steeply up the spine of Sheep Down, offering good views left over Knollend Down and continues straight on following some racing gallops on the right. The grass downland here is a haven for skylarks and in late spring/early summer, their song follows you all the way. There is also an abundance of lapwings, distracting you from their nesting areas with their individual flight and sound.

Sometime on, the track you are following bends right. You should leave it here to continue straight on along a less defined track, signposted as a bridleway. There are even better views here, almost 180 degrees, over the surrounding countryside. After some distance, the bridleway meets another set of gallops coming in from the left. As before, you should continue straight on where ahead of you and just visible is the Ridgeway, distinguishable by the walkers and mountain bikers dressed in the latest garb.

The track together with the gallops, bends gently left and passes a line of pine trees on your left. For just a short spell here, our route actually passes into Oxfordshire. Soon after, you will meet the Ridgeway on your right. (For the history of the Ridgeway, see "In Giants' Footsteps"). Turn left along the Ridgeway which at this point traverses East Hendred Down (187m) and head for some trees in the distance. On a clear day, you will be treated to some magnificent views right over the Vale of the White Horse, dominated by the large cooling towers of Didcot power station. Immediately below you, are the stark buildings of the sometimes controversial Harwell Atomic Energy research establishment.

Stay on the Ridgeway until you meet a crossing track and parking area in front of a narrow copse. The copse hides Scutchamer Knob, a Saxon burial mound.

Scutchamer Knob (OS. 456850 Map 174). *Before the copse, the barrow which is said to have been seventyseven feet high, was an important landmark. The name of the barrow is reportedly derived from the Saxon King, Cwicchelm. Personally, I find it hard to see how, as far more likely is the name of the hill on which it stands, Cuckhamsley Hill. Scutchamer Knob is also said to mark the spot where the famous Battle of Ashdown between Alfred's Saxons and the Danes took place. The battle was one of the biggest and bloodiest to have ever taken place on English soil, with thousands being left for dead on the downs. The Saxons were the eventual victors after Alfred had surprised the Danes by personally leading a charge into their midst. The barrow is only one of several suggested sites where the battle is said to have taken place, writers of the day tell us that the battle "raged on a hill top around a lone thorn tree". Unfortunately, this landmark would have disappeared centuries ago and until a farmer ploughs up a mass grave, the site of the battle will remain in dispute for years to come.*

Turn left onto the crossing track which is marked as a public right of way and leads south in the direction of the Berkshire Downs, visible in the distance. It also follows another set of gallops on the left. Stay on the track which runs downhill and ignore all turnings off until you eventually meet a lane. Turn right along the lane taking note of the blue arrows marking the way - this indicates a local cycling route. After approximately three hundred metres, you will arrive at "Lands End Cottage" on your right. Cross the road and join a track opposite the cottage, which leads uphill and is signposted as a byway.

The track leads gently up the side of Old Down, heading south. It is known as Old Street and probably gave its name to the down and not the other way around, as this is an ancient track which started life around the same time as the Ridgeway, which it meets a few miles north. The track is lined in places by the remains of an old hedgerow. As you progress, you will enjoy increasingly good views over the Berkshire Downs and behind to the Ridgeway. To your right, the water tower in the distance marks Farnborough, our next destination.

On nearing the top, the hedgerow becomes thicker and shortly after, you should ignore a bridleway off to the left to continue straight on. The track continues through a strip of woodland which in late spring/early summer is carpeted by a mass of vibrant bluebells, of a density I have never seen elsewhere. The going here can be extremely muddy, so much so that I wondered at one point whether to advise bringing your bathers! Fortunately, there is a narrow winding path adjacent to the track, which can be used to avoid the worst of the mud.

Eventually the track meets a crossing track where you should turn right along a signposted public right of way. The right of way continues for a short distance almost back on yourself, before bending left to head towards the village of Farnborough. After a short distance, you should ignore another track off to the left to continue ahead. The route is lined by hedgerows, giving way in places to afford superb views across the downs.

You will eventually reach a wide crossing track which you should ignore to continue ahead and immediately after, you will meet a fork. Take the right hand fork, a path which runs between banks, where as a guide, you should be able to see the church tower at Farnborough ahead of you. Follow the path to soon lead downhill into a farm yard and continue straight on to meet a lane beside a somewhat hidden pond on your right. Ahead of you are the buildings of "Upper Farm". Turn left along the lane and follow it to the church, passing "The Old Rectory", a house of Dutch style on your right.

Farnborough (OS. 435819 Map 174) *sits high on the downs (218m / 735ft) and is the highest point on the walk. Its solid church tower, though not great in height, because of its position marks Farnborough for miles around. Farnborough's existence probably stems from its advantageous position, being high up and close to two ancient routes, Old Street and the Ridgeway. Remains from successive early inhabitants have been found in the fields surrounding the village. More recently, the village was a welcome stop on the old packhorse route between Hungerford and Oxford.*

The church dates from the 12th century, the tower being added in the 15th century. Inside, you will find a colourful window in memory of the Poet Lauriet, Sir John Betjamin. The window was placed here by "The Friends of Friendless Churches" and was designed by Betjamin's friend, John Piper. Sir John Betjamin moved to Farnborough with his wife in 1945. They made their home at "The Old Rectory", the Dutch style house which you passed on entering the village. The house was built in the 18th century and Betjamin's wife in a letter to a friend, revealed some apprehension about living here. Explaining her concerns, she wrote, "It is a dream of beauty, but has no water - no light and is falling down and needs six servants, so it will probably kill us in the end". On certain days in summer, the garden is open to the public. If you are fortunate enough to be passing on such a day, you could do a lot worse than take a privileged look around.

Just before the church, ignore two footpaths on your left and continue to follow the lane through the village. Pass "The Old Post Office" and ignore two more footpaths on the left.

On nearing the end of the village, take a road left beside a small green signposted to Lilley and Newbury. Just after joining, look out for a farm on the left selling eggs, meats and vegetables and in particular, note its distinctive "piggy" weather vein. Stay on the lane which begins to descend and ignore a footpath left and a small road on the right. Just after, take a signposted footpath on your right and follow the path across a field along a line of telegraph poles. Approximately two thirds of the way across (at the fifth telegraph pole), bear diagonally right and head for the now visible footpath sign at the far side of the field.

Leave the field to meet a road, the B4494. Turn right along the road and then first left along a small road more of a lane, signposted to Brightwalton and Chaddleworth. Follow the lane until it later bends right beside a house. Here you should leave it and take a track ahead marked as a byway, passing to the left of the house. Follow the byway for a short distance and as the field on your left ends, take a track left, also a byway. This descends to eventually meet another track on the right opposite some old farm buildings, marked on the map as "Lower Barn". Take the track right which initially leads uphill.

After some distance, ignore a track coming in from the right and continue straight on, with the prominent spire of Brightwalton church now in view, to eventually meet a lane. Cross the lane and continue following another lane ahead, where you should ignore a footpath on your right leading to "Manor Farmhouse". Shortly after, take the first lane on your right to walk between the houses of Brightwalton village.

i
✝
■
🚶‍♂️🚶‍♀️

Brightwalton (OS. 428793 Map 174), *hidden away amongst the downs, has a mixture of old and new which blend reasonably well. During the holidays, the main street is alive with the noise of children playing, a refreshing sound lost in so many of our villages. At the western end of the village standing amongst picture postcard cottages, is the church. Like the church at Fawley (see "The Lambourn Lunge"), it was designed by the Victorian architect, Street. There are still a few remaining signs of the original Norman church which stood on this site, including a brass to John Newman (1517).*

Following the Battle of Newbury, Roundheads and Royalists met in a skirmish in some nearby woods. Skeletons of the unfortunate victims of this encounter were found in the garden at the village inn. The inn itself has sadly since closed.

Halfway through the village, look out for two signposted footpaths opposite each other, on the left and right respectively. Take the footpath left, a track which runs between gardens to soon meet a small play area and stile beside a farm gate. Cross the stile and go straight across a field following the left hand perimeter. As you progress, look carefully through the trees on your left and you will see part of the Brightwalton Light Railway. This is a private railway built by an enthusiast in his garden. On certain days in summer, it is open to the general public.

i

At the corner of the field, cross another stile into the next field and continue ahead along a well defined path. At the far side, on meeting a lane opposite "Malthouse Farm", turn right to follow the lane into Brightwalton Green. At a "T" junction, turn left in the direction of the sign to Chaddleworth, Leckhampstead and Boxford. Pass the "Wesleyan Chapel" on your right and as the road later bends right in front of a small green, leave it and carry straight on in the direction of the sign for Newbury. The green here once housed a well which was two hundred and eightythree feet deep. For safety's sake it has since been filled in.

i

After approximately twenty paces, turn left onto a signposted footpath which runs across the centre of a field. At the far side, continue ahead to follow the right hand perimeter of the next field. There are good views left here of the Berkshire Downs and Brightwalton church. At the corner of the field, carry straight on to join a sometimes hidden narrow hedged footpath. Follow this to reach the drive way of a picturesque cottage. Turn right in front of the cottage and follow the drive way down to meet a lane.

Turn right along the lane to soon meet a "T" junction. Turn left and follow another lane downhill and just before reaching the bottom of the valley, turn right onto a signposted footpath. This takes you across the centre of a field. At the far side, go over a stile into the next field, where you should continue ahead along the right hand perimeter. Go over a stile at the field end, through a small strip of scrub and over a second stile to arrive at a farm track.

Turn right along the track, also a byway and follow this through "Cotswold Farm", to continue uphill between hedgerows. Soon after, the track forks and you should take the right hand fork, still marked as a byway. Your way is now through open woodland where you should ignore a track coming in from the left. Stay on the byway thereafter as it bends left and continue ahead, later ignoring a signposted footpath on your right. The byway eventually leads you to Leckhampstead village. Turn left along a lane to arrive at the village green.

Leckhampstead (OS. 439764 Map 174), *sitting high above the Newbury to Wantage road, has one of the most unusual war memorials to be found in the country. Standing boldly at the centre of the village green, the memorial is obelisk shaped with a clock at its top. On closer inspection, you will see the hands of the clock are in fact bayonets, the minutes machine gun ammunition and the Roman numerals, rifle ammunition. Slightly more obvious, are the shell cases which surround the base and support a chain taken from an old battleship.*

For some welcome refreshment, the village unlike many others in the area still has a pub. This is "The Stag", a Morland pub. It is an unpretentious hostelry selling good honest beer and traditional home cooked food.

Follow the lane round to the right of the green and memorial to soon arrive at the village pub, "The Stag". If you do not wish to visit the pub, then our route is to take a turning left just before the pub, passing through the car park of the village hall, to join a signposted public footpath at the far side.

The footpath runs across a field and follows a line of telegraph poles. At the bottom of the field cross a road, the B4494 and continue ahead now going uphill and still following the line of telegraph poles. At the top of the field take time to look back, catch your breath and enjoy the views across to Brightwalton church to the north and Beacon Hill, south.

The War Memorial Leckhampstead

To continue, pass through a gap in the hedge beside one of the telegraph poles, go over a stile and through a strip of woodland. You should then go over two stiles in succession to enter a field on your right. Once in the field, turn left and follow the left hand perimeter to the far side. The spire of Peasemore church, our next destination, is now clearly visible ahead to your left.

At the far side of the field, pass through a gate and follow a track ahead, passing a barn, to go through another gate and arrive at the hamlet of Hillgreen. Turn left along a lane where you may wish to follow a narrow path on the right hand grass verge, and first right along another lane signposted to Beedon and Chieveley. Approximately two hundred metres up this lane, take a signposted footpath left which leads diagonally right across a field. The buildings in the distance here mark the outskirts of Peasemore village, the large white building is the pub.

Leave the field to arrive at a narrow lane over which trees meet to, in summer, form a welcome shady tunnel and a myriad of greens. Between April and June, the lane is bordered by a dazzling display of the white flowering cow parsley. From here you have a choice, you can either cross the road and follow the footpath diagonally left, which leads you to a garden through which you must pass and turn left to rejoin the lane, turning right to arrive at the centre of Peasemore village. Alternatively, you can simply turn left along this pretty lane which, after a short distance, enters Peasemore beside a converted barn. The choice is yours, but unless you have a deep desire to cross someone's garden, I recommend the lane which is an equally if not more attractive way, to reach Peasemore. Both routes will lead you to a "T" junction in front of the village church.

Peasemore (OS. 458771 Map 174) *has the feel of having been here for a long time. Old flint walls separate deep thatched cottages from shady lanes, with an impressive church and noisy resident rooks watching over all. Like Farnborough, the village probably grew with the creation of ancient routes across the Berkshire Downs. The first known settlement here was Saxon and the Saxon church was dedicated to a Saxon saint, St. Peada, son of King Penda of Mercia. Unfortunately, this saint was never recognised by the Christian church and despite local feeling which favoured the Saxon saint, the current church is dedicated to St. Barnabas.*

The Saxon church was later replaced by a more solid Norman structure which stood for seven hundred and fifty years until 1842, when the over enthusiastic Victorians demolished it to build the church which stands today. They did however, leave the tower which had in 1737, been added to the Norman church by a charitable local resident, William Coward. The Victorians added a spire to the top of the tower and this is now a landmark for miles around.

Little remains of the Norman church, much of the masonry having been used in the building of local houses. One relic however, that has survived sits on a straddle stone (a mushroom shaped stone once used to support a stack of hay) beside the church porch. This is one of the gargoyles and was discovered being used as a stepping stone to a stile on the footpath opposite, a short cut across Princes Meadow to "The Fox and Hounds".

If you scout the flint walls along the lanes, you may find the "lucky hole". This is a deep recess in one of the flints. Villagers would often leave a small gift here for the next passer-by which could be anything from fruits from the hedgerow to a few pence or a button. If you find the hole, please help preserve tradition by leaving something for the next person. Something else worth searching for is the village pub, "The Fox and Hounds". The easiest and shortest way to get to it, is to take the footpath opposite the church. A popular pub, "The Fox and Hounds" attracts trade from many of the surrounding villages, by serving some wholesome meals in its restaurant and offering some respectable ales.

Apart from the pub, the village is worth exploring for its own sake. It has a charm unmatched by many of its neighbours and to save a few minutes by simply passing through, would be a great shame.

The stone stile at Peasemore

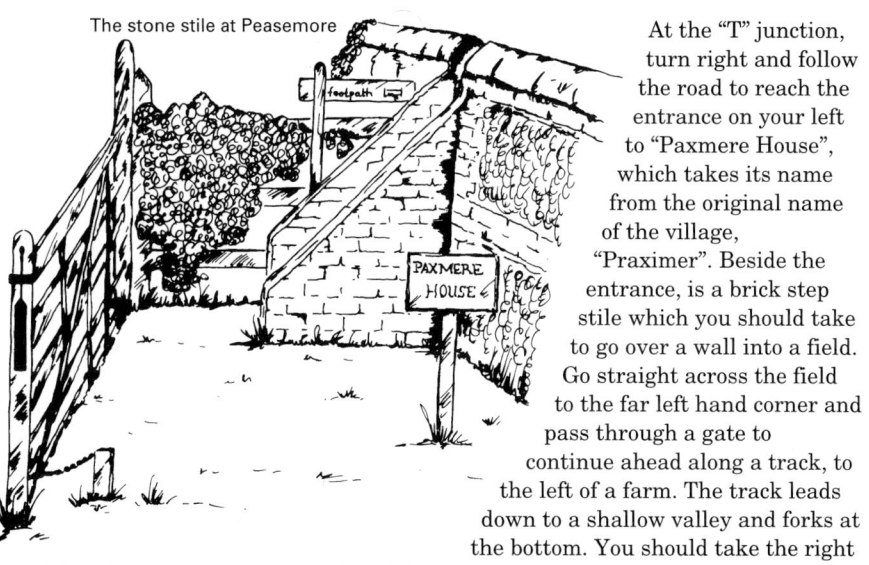

At the "T" junction, turn right and follow the road to reach the entrance on your left to "Paxmere House", which takes its name from the original name of the village, "Praximer". Beside the entrance, is a brick step stile which you should take to go over a wall into a field. Go straight across the field to the far left hand corner and pass through a gate to continue ahead along a track, to the left of a farm. The track leads down to a shallow valley and forks at the bottom. You should take the right hand fork to go uphill passing to the right of a copse.

Thereafter, the track takes you once again onto high ground where there are superb views in just about every direction. After a short distance, the track bends left and you should leave it here to carry straight on along the right hand perimeter of a field, to soon go downhill. At the far side of the field, turn right for a few paces and then left to meet a track. This is Old Street. Turn left along the track and shortly after, ignore a footpath off to your right. After this, follow the track between thick hedgerows to, after approximately three quarters of a mile, arrive at a lane by a small clearing used by the council as a gravel store.

Cross the lane and continue ahead along a track the other side, signposted as a byway. The ancient track continues to run north heading for the Ridgeway. As you continue, sometimes through thick mud, look out for a round barrow in a field to your right, just discernible through the dense hedgerow.

Beedon Round Barrow (OS. 467786 Map 174) *was once believed by locals to be inhabited by fairies. When archeologists came to excavate the barrow in 1815, they had tremendous trouble obtaining permission from the landowner, who feared revenge from the fairies and the ghosts of those interred. Bribery eventually overcame superstition and the dig began. That day, a tremendous storm broke and the villagers, fearing it was the wrath of the dead, attempted to prevent further digging. One of the labourers was so scared that he left, despite the promise of extra money.*

Eventually, the barrow was excavated and the storm passed leaving everyone in one piece. Inside, evidence of cremation was found along with an incense cup and a bronze dagger. A gold coffin which the locals also believed lay inside, was never found.

Sometime on, the track forks and you should take the right hand fork, still signposted as a byway, thereby leaving Old Street to join another ancient track, Green Lane **(OS. 466791)**. Soon after the fork, you should ignore a track off to the right, also signposted as a byway which leads to Stanmore.

The track then runs between fields and thereafter, passes to the right of Redlane

Wood. As the wood ends, you will pass a small cottage on your left and should ignore a drive way off to the right to carry straight on. The byway will then take you initially along the left hand perimeter of a field and approximately half way across, between hedgerows. After a short distance, you should go over a crossing track to continue ahead, going downhill between banks as well as hedgerows. N.B. If you end up following a track directly into another field, you will need to retrace your steps to find the track which runs between banks.

Eventually, the track narrows and you should pass through a metal gate into a field. Continue ahead along the right hand perimeter of the field where to your left, are the ruins of an old barn. This is marked on the map as "Woolvers Barn". Pass through a gap in the fencing into the next field where as before, you should follow the right hand perimeter. The views ahead now in the distance are of the Ridgeway.

At the far end of the field, pass through a metal gate to reach a crossing track. Go over the crossing track and continue ahead, still following the signposted byway. You will shortly meet a turning left signposted as a public bridleway, which you should take. After approximately thirty metres, turn right onto another signposted public bridleway, which climbs slowly uphill. If your legs are aching you can gain some relief in the knowledge that this is the last ascent on the walk. The climb is worth the pain and at the top you will enjoy a final view of the Berkshire Downs, which stretch as far as the hills above the Goring Gap. Thereafter, you can begin a welcome descent to West Ilsley.

As you near the bottom of the hill a large house will come into view on your right. This is "Hodcott House", the premier racing establishment of this part of the downs. Many famous horses are stabled here, some of them owned by the Queen. Continue to follow the track downhill and just before some outhouses to "Hodcott House", follow the track as it bends left and then right. You should ignore a track left here signposted as a public footpath.

The track you are following skirts the perimeter of the house to eventually meet a tarmacced drive. Turn left along the drive which later bends right, just after some stables on your left. You should ignore a gravel track on your left here and continue for a few paces more to take the next turning left, a fenced footpath which runs between the first houses of West Ilsley.

Follow the footpath to soon arrive at the main street of West Ilsley. Cross the road, turn left and follow the road back through the centre of the village, passing the General Stores and church. Thereafter, you will arrive at "The Harrow" pub, our starting point. If you still have the energy to read whilst enjoying that well earned drink at "The Harrow", I will finish by telling you a little about West Ilsley.

West Ilsley (OS. 475825 Map 174) *is often overshadowed by its better known neighbour, East Ilsley, overrun by tourists and walkers at weekends. This is to West Ilsley's advantage, as its attraction is its peaceful position sheltered from the winds in the folds of the downs. The village is larger than most, served surprisingly by a relatively small church. Amongst its rectors was the Italien, Marc Antonio de Dominis. He was appointed rector here by James I after fleeing Rome in 1616, to avoid punishment by the Roman church for his scientific views. James I also made him Dean of Windsor. Marc Antonio however, disappointed in not getting more, insulted the King by publicly detracting everything he had written that had upset the church. With the promise of a pardon from Pope Gregory, he hastily returned to Rome.*

All was not forgiven by Rome however, and instead of a welcome, Marc Antonio was imprisoned in the fortress of St. Angelo. Shortly after, he died, some say of poison. The wrath of the religious fanatics he had insulted was not appeased even after death and his body was later dug up and at a public meeting, burned along with his writings.

A later rector, Dr. Godfrey Goodman, fared little better when he was stripped of his wealth by the Parliamentarians for entertaining Charles Stuart at the Rectory here. Dr. Goodman tried to regain favour by later dedicating a sermon on the Trinity to Oliver Cromwell.

Apart from agriculture, West Ilsley's other important industry used to be brewing, once having two breweries to boast of. One of them was run by the Morland family at "West Ilsley House". Today, the breweries have gone, but Morland still lives on and "The Harrow", a free house, ensures that good ales are still sold in the village. The pub has changed greatly since I first passed this way in the mid-70's, whilst walking the Ridgeway. Then, it was a simple affair with the minimum of comfort, except for the friendly welcome of the landlord. Now, a woody bar with character and walls covered with pictures of successful horses trained in the village, is the setting in which you can enjoy a well deserved drink. An imaginative menu includes a wide range of cheeses which you can also buy to take home with you. In summer, you can enjoy your drink outside whilst watching the cricket or slightly more interesting, the noisy variety of animals in the pub garden.

Enjoying your drink, I hope you will remember the day's exertions with pleasure and will join me for some further adventures.

ACCOMMODATION

The Swan, East Ilsley. Tel: 0635 28238
Approximately one and a half miles from the walk, this is a pleasant inn at the centre of a village of outstanding beauty.

Langley Farm, Beedon. Tel: 0635 248222
Two miles from the walk, this is a lovely Victorian manor house attached to a working farm in the middle of the Berkshire Downs.

Youth Hostel, The Court Hill Ridgeway Centre YHA. Tel: 02357 60253
Six and a half miles from the walk, this is a purpose built hostel from the reconstruction of four barns. The hostel is in a beautiful position with views over the Vale of the White Horse. The grounds include a wood where you can camp and has a barbecue area.

Camping and Caravanning, Gatehampton Farm, Goring. Tel: 0491 872894
Ten miles from the walk, this is an informal site on the bank of the river Thames. Facilities are minimal, but then that is the beauty of the location. A pleasant walk takes you to the attractions of Goring itself.

SOME FURTHER ADVENTURES

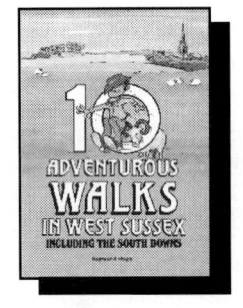

10 MORE ADVENTUROUS WALKS IN SURREY

10 ADVENTUROUS WALKS IN THE SOUTH CHILTERNS

KEEP UP TO DATE

If you would like a full list and to be kept updated on all the outdoor publications available from Morning Mist, please send a postcard with your name and address to Marketing, Morning Mist Publications, PO Box 108, Reigate, Surrey RH2 9YP.